PRAISE FOR
THE REVENUE ENGINE

"Out with theory, in with action!" Those were my sentiments after reading Kara Smith Brown's playbook for success in *The Revenue Engine*. I've always felt that Marketing overcomplicates the "x's and o's," but Kara provides practical advice which effectively relocates traditional marketing from an expense line into a measurable revenue generator. If increasing revenues is the goal, this is the playbook!

— Jack Daly
Serial entrepreneur, CEO coach, and best-selling author

As a long-time advocate for smart entrepreneurial growth, I see *The Revenue Engine* by Kara Smith Brown as a resource for any entrepreneur or executive looking to scale their B2B business effectively. Her book aligns with the methodologies we teach at the Growth Institute and Scaling Up, offering actionable strategies that are crucial for businesses aiming to navigate the complexities of market expansion and revenue generation. It's a useful addition to the entrepreneurial toolkit, blending practical wisdom with strategic guidance.

—Verne Harnish
Founder of Entrepreneurs' Organization (EO) and author of
Scaling Up (Rockefeller Habits 2.0)

In *The Revenue Engine*, Kara Brown provides a clear and actionable framework that every B2B company can benefit from. Her strategies are not just theories; they are proven methods that drive growth.

— Andy Lark
Global B2B CMO, builder of billion dollar startups, coach, and advisor to leading B2B brands

Generating attention for your company, product, or idea isn't about spending tons of money or knocking on the most doors. It's about understanding buyers, sharing good news about what you do and how you do it, and building fans. Kara shows you how with tons of examples of success to learn from.

— David Meerman Scott
Wall Street Journal *best-selling author of twelve books, including* The New Rules of Marketing and PR

Kara is a *true leader* in her field… she walks the talk in every way. In her new book *The Revenue Engine* she breaks down the complex into simple, digestible, and most importantly *actionable* parts. If you have found yourself stuck in your business Kara, with real world experience not just hypothesis, brings to these pages the instruction manual for creating an engine you can rely on!

— Andy Bailey
Serial entrepreneur, speaker, and constant adventurer who has built two successful coaching businesses: Petra Coach and Boundless.me

THE REVENUE ENGINE

Blake —
I loved hearing the
GenLog Story on the FreightPod.
Always Be Closing!

Kara Smith Born

THE REVENUE ENGINE

ENGINE

FUELING
A B2B
HIGH-OCTANE
PIPELINE

KARA
SMITH
BROWN

Advantage | Books

Published by Advantage Books, Charleston, South Carolina.
An imprint of Advantage Media.

ADVANTAGE is a registered trademark, and the Advantage colophon is a trademark of Advantage Media Group, Inc.

Printed in the United States of America.

10 9 8 7 6 5 4 3 2 1

ISBN: 978-1-64225-909-4 (Paperback)
ISBN: 978-1-64225-908-7 (eBook)

Library of Congress Control Number: 2024918671

Cover design by Kris McCarthy.
Layout design by Ruthie Wood.

This publication is designed to provide accurate and authoritative information in regard to the subject matter covered. It is sold with the understanding that the publisher is not engaged in rendering legal, accounting, or other professional services. If legal advice or other expert assistance is required, the services of a competent professional person should be sought.

Advantage Books is an imprint of Advantage Media Group. Advantage Media helps busy entrepreneurs, CEOs, and leaders write and publish a book to grow their business and become the authority in their field. Advantage authors comprise an exclusive community of industry professionals, idea-makers, and thought leaders. For more information go to **advantagemedia.com**.

CONTENTS

ACKNOWLEDGMENTS

With gratitude and love:

To Eric Brown:

The love of my life, the man of my dreams, and the captain of my ship. Your steadfast support, limitless patience, and belief in me have been the rock on which I am privileged to build. This book would never have come to life without you by my side.

To John and Diane Smith:

The unwavering encouragement, leadership, and solid foundation you've given me have been the bedrock of this journey. Your wisdom has illuminated my path, and your support shapes every decision I make.

To Katherine and Elizabeth Brown:

You are my greatest inspiration and my life's purest joy. This book is a tribute to the dreams you will always chase and the endless possibilities that lie ahead of you.

To the team at LeadCoverage:

Your dedication and hard work have made this book a reality. I'm deeply grateful for your support, resourcefulness, and tireless efforts. Together, we've turned an idea into something tangible and impactful.

For every "marketing girl" out there finding her way in the world: This one's for you. May these pages empower you to claim your space, earn a seat at the table, and if necessary—build your own table.

FOREWORD

BY SANGRAM VAJRE, COFOUNDER AND CEO OF GTM PARTNERS

I first heard about Kara Brown through the Atlanta business network. I was cofounder of Terminus, the first ABM platform, and she had started LeadCoverage, a B2B consultancy taking the logistics world by storm.

She and her team were offering demand gen strategies that actually worked! And she could measure the impact of her efforts on the pipeline. Not many marketing consultants make it much beyond vanity metrics like engagement and page visits.

What I heard again and again was that everyone was begging Kara to expand beyond the supply chain industry because her methods could help so many other companies.

But she always shrugged, and said, "Logistics is a two-trillion-dollar industry in the US alone. We'll branch out once we've taught all the forwarders, brokers, freight tech, and carriers how to get value out of their go-to-market (GTM) approach. We have plenty of work to keep us busy!" You'll recognize her voice in that comment as you read the book and hear the stories and case studies she includes here.

That's why I was so excited to read the first draft of this book. In the following pages, she explains the foolproof lead generation framework she created to help so many companies achieve efficient growth. Now she's offering it to any B2B company in any industry with the will and curiosity to try it out.

Let's face it, B2B companies need all the help we can get. We've been obsessed with the relentless pursuit of growth at any cost over the last few decades. But it's becoming clear that this approach is unsustainable because what so many B2B companies are doing just isn't working.

Our GTM strategies have to evolve if they're going to have a measurable impact on revenue.

We need to move away from growth at all costs and focus on efficient growth.

The brutal truth is that GTM and B2B demand generation is *hard*.[1]

- **The B2B buying process is complex.** Eighty percent of B2B companies have buying committees that influence software purchasing decisions with twenty-two distinct roles which are involved in the process.

- **Contracts are shorter.** More than half of software contracts are for fewer than six months and only 11 percent last more than two years.

- **The importance of the vendor's sales team is declining.** Sixty-eight percent of B2B buyers only involve the vendor's sales team at the last stage of the buying process.

- **Vendors need to show value quickly.** Buyers list simple implementation, a quicker return on investment (ROI), and ease of use as their three most important considerations.

- **Renewals are getting trickier.** Only 45 percent of software buyers renew without consideration. Fifty-three percent research and contemplate alternatives when a product is up for renewal.

So you're not alone if you're feeling like GTM is harder than ever at a time when we have more tech to sort out, smaller budgets, and siloed departments.

As companies navigate the ever-evolving landscape of GTM strategies, there's a clear shift from traditional approaches to more innovative and integrated methodologies that have measurable impact.

Kara's book leads the way, and here are some of my takeaways:

1. **Marketing must be measurable.** No one is going to listen to you if you can't show your impact. This is why Kara teaches strategies like "Commercial PR" that focus on measurable outcomes and data-driven strategies instead of just press releases and feel-good puff pieces.

2. **The GTM team must own the measurement.** Using the three Vs–volume, velocity, and value–the GTM team must be able to show leadership that they have a command of the business and prove what they're doing is working or that they have a plan to fix it if it isn't.

3. **We must change the way we think.** This work, and especially the three-by-three framework Kara teaches (methodologies, funnels, and measurement), is about more than just generating leads and building pipeline. Marketing the business is no longer enough. We need to understand the business of marketing.

4. **Success depends on strategic thinking with actual execution.** Plenty of business books talk strategy with no practical application, and plenty of books share tips and tricks without any underlying philosophy. This book shows you the strategy but really gives very practical, detailed advice on how to *do* things. And with most of the suggestions in this book, you can start right away. You don't need to wait.

This book is a shortcut to efficient pipeline generation for any B2B company, giving you frameworks that took Kara fifteen years to create. The humor and generosity with which she shares her experience and methods make it clear she wants to spare others the trial and error she experienced early in her career.

She is lighting the path for others who are following in her footsteps. She's inviting you to have a seat at the table she had to set herself.

Whether you are new to marketing, an industry veteran, or a C-level leader, this book has time-tested strategies that will improve your GTM efforts. And some great stories, too, including case studies and personal anecdotes.

So pull up a chair. Learn new ways to tell your story across the full customer life cycle in ways that can demonstrate results. Make the most of your seat at the table!

INTRODUCTION

I was the "marketing girl."

Fresh out of college and into the early years of my career, I was building a solid résumé in the B2B marketing space with jobs in the original freight tech start-up, a private equity–backed warehouse roll-up, and a garbage broker. I stayed in the heavily industrial, B2B world and my roles and experience expanded. But in these male-dominated industries, even as one of the few women in a leadership position, no matter my title, or the size of my team or contribution, I was always the "marketing girl."

In 2006, I was one of the first employees at Echo Global Logistics. In fact, I was the entire marketing department. Echo Global Logistics was a superfast-growing company with a sales team that multiplied by thirty to fifty people a month. The IT team was growing nearly that fast, along with a credit team, a finance team, and many others. And then there was me: the marketing department of one, my own little entity. And let's just be honest, I didn't really know what I was doing.

In many ways, that wasn't a bad thing, because, to sink or swim, I had to learn on the job. Unlike my colleagues, who were hired into larger teams that were developing processes and procedures to handle growth and scale, monthly KPIs for the "marketing girl" were pretty fuzzy, so it freed me up to learn and try new things.

Doug Waggoner, CEO of Echo, put together an excellent team of executives to scale that business as fast as he did. Nearly 3,000 percent growth in three years that resulted in an IPO on October 9, 2009. (The company has since gone private at a market cap of $3.8 billion, and as of this writing, Doug Waggoner is still the CEO.) I watched as this team worked together, made decisions, and achieved incredible success. It left an indelible impression on me, as did Doug. I stayed as close to him and the leadership team as I could. Every time I had a chance to be in the room with Doug, I learned something. He spoke with confidence about the economics of supply chain and its macroeconomic impact globally. I was continuously learning about what was happening in the larger ecosystem when I was with him. He's still that way.

When I had the opportunity to be in *that* room with Doug and his leadership team, it felt electric. This is where things were happening. Conversations were smart. The decisions made were big. And the value was outsized. *Big* things weren't happening in my little world of marketing. I could make all the sell sheets I wanted, but it wasn't going to mean anything in that room. And I wanted to be in *that* room.

Early in my career, I had the first of what would be many "lessons learned" moments. I asked our graphic designer to pull together changes to our brand and tagline. I believed I was delivering value. I had visions of the leadership team being blown out of the water. I would get smiles and nods. I already had my customized executive chair picked out in my mind's eye. That seat at the table was mine.

So I called a meeting and invited the entire leadership team. Where I got the confidence (it was more likely naivete) to do this baffles me today. The day of the meeting I sat with the PowerPoint presentation the graphic designer created for me called up, and I started my presentation.

I went through slide after slide, showing the new logo variations we created and walked through the new tagline we were going to use and advertisements we were going to run to showcase them both. I was incredibly proud of the creative work we had done.

Five minutes into my presentation, someone interrupted me by saying, "What are we doing here?"

I told him that this was important work. We needed to have this brand work done.

He didn't agree.

"We all have better things to do with our time, including you. Don't ever interrupt the work we're doing with anything like this again," he said. With that, he and the leadership team left the room. They were leaving me and my silly little meeting about branding to go and make money. Which is all they wanted me to do too. They wanted me to help them drive revenue and I gave them a color palette.

It could have been mortifying for me had I let it. But in that moment, something clicked. They were right. Pretty pictures and taglines were never going to get me a seat at the table. Those things just weren't important to the leadership team because they wouldn't show a direct impact to the bottom line.

Clearly I wasn't going to make that mistake again. No one was going to listen to the "marketing girl" if I didn't have something substantial to say. Had I brought them into that meeting with a point of view on how we're going to measure our go-to-market (GTM), it would've been an entirely different conversation.

I wanted to be a part of that team, on that executive leadership level. I wanted to be at the table, contributing to the decision-making, adding value, and growing the business. I was going to need to deliver the math.

I also needed to provide a *point of view* on how that math impacted the business. This C-suite craved math. It required math if I had any hope of grabbing that seat at the table.

As soon as I left that meeting, my insatiable curiosity about math and measurement kicked in. I began reading everything I could get my hands on related to "funnel" math and deltas. I explored Harvard Business School frameworks and models. I also searched for and could not find a B2B marketing playbook on delivering value.

The first thing I learned: It wasn't enough for me to understand math; I had to be able to *explain* it to the executive leadership team (ELT) because marketing math is not like other math. It's nuanced, part science and part art, with matrixed dependencies and layered impact. And I had to be able to explain it in a way that the executive team could understand.

There was another catch: The ELT had to be able to see it in *one slide*. As the marketer at a B2B company, you don't get a whole Power-Point deck. I know that now! You don't get a section of someone else's deck. You get *one slide* in the deck. One slide to explain your point, to provide evidence for your point, and to get alignment and approval. At that point, I had yet to see this done successfully—anywhere. This may explain why the average CMO tenure is forty months.[2] It's often far less. In fact, in 2022, 30 percent of CMOs in one marketing sector were new to their positions—less than twelve months on the job.[3]

In my career I have often been allowed one slide to present—and had to show my value in a single moment. The pressure was and is on to show marketing's efficacy, effectiveness, and contribution to the bottom line. But with my research not turning up any sort of B2B marketing playbook for this, where would anyone go to learn how to show what needed to be shown? Where does someone start to prove marketing's worth?

This led me to learn a very important lesson early on: No marketer can do it alone. I was going to have to work with other people in the organization to make this happen. Luckily, Sangram Vajre, a friend and luminary in the space, and others have made clear, in a nutshell, that marketing's job is to serve sales as a part of the revenue team. Great marketing doesn't happen in a vacuum. I was going to need to join forces with sales.

A seat in the "room where it happens" was my goal, and not too long after that fateful meeting I had called with leadership to talk about my logos, I had achieved that goal. Within three years I had proved myself, and leadership asked me to participate in preparing Echo Global Logistics for an initial public offering (IPO). In fact, my name is on the company's 2009 IPO [NYSE: ECHO] press release.

The first step to partnering with sales was to actually *care* very much about the sales team's success. If I didn't focus on and show the value of sales-driven initiatives, I would be reduced to the "marketing" box. I would remain the "marketing girl."

To be sales' partner, I had to participate at every level: pipeline review, spiff planning, pricing decisions, and unit economic product discussions, and most importantly, I had to show the *volume* of the leads, the *value* of the leads, and the *velocity* of the leads that were going to the sales team. To keep the seat at the table, I needed a point of view on how marketing was contributing to revenue. And I knew it would have very little to do with brand colors or a snappy tagline.

THE MARKETING ROLE PARADOX

There are two types of B2B marketing roles.

- Branding: Beautiful logos and pretty pictures, colors and design, brochures, and websites. How a brand is perceived in the marketplace is super important, but it isn't my strong suit, and it didn't get me a seat at the table.

- Demand Gen: Data-driven and results-focused using hypothesis testing, goals, and clear Key Performance Indicators (KPIs) meant to drive ROI. In other words, relevant math.

Brand and demand gen motions are both necessary. In my experience, only one is meeting regularly with executive leadership.

As the founder of LeadCoverage, a B2B GTM consultancy, I've spent years developing insights into demand generation tactics, testing them and optimizing them. I've focused on all the pieces of the B2B conversion cycle, including MarTech stack building (customer relationship management [CRM]/automation), sales/marketing operations and enablement, inbound/outbound content, SEO/SEM, social conversion, public relations (PR), and measurement. And throughout my career, I developed a simple but effective framework you'll read about in this book.

If I had had a book like this back when I was figuring out what to do next at Echo Global Logistics, I would have asked the leadership team to come to a very different meeting and my career may have had an entirely different trajectory. This book is meant to be a manual of sorts. A playbook to follow.

Yes, my background is supply chain, heavy industrial, and tech. Don't worry if that isn't your vertical: the framework is for *every B2B marketer* who isn't the pretty-pictures-and-logo type. It's for the marketer who delivers real results and to fuel a B2B pipeline. This book is also for the leaders—CEOs and CROs—who want to understand precisely how a well-executed marketing strategy can deliver the measurable marketing impact and ROI they may not know how to ask for.

It took me fifteen years to figure it all out—to have a methodology and point of view so clear that, well, I could write a book about it. This book is the result of years of trial and error, proving a model and developing a framework, then putting it all into an actionable approach.

GO-TO-MARKET (GTM)

One of my favorite authors and friends in this space is Sangram Vajre. He has written multiple books on account-based marketing and the adopted term, go-to-market (GTM) function. Vajre and his coauthor Bryan Brown's book *MOVE: The 4-Question Go-to-Market Framework* has helped me crystallize my own framework. I use the words go-to-market differently than they do, but I like their definition: "GTM is a transformational process for accelerating your path to market where high-performing revenue teams (marketing, sales, and customer success) deliver a connected customer experience and every touchpoint reinforces the brand, values, and vision of your company."[4] Vajre and Brown are clear that GTM is not a singular strategy, but an iterative process that enables the larger strategy.

I'd like to think that this book is a how-to guide and extension of this framework made into a playbook for the B2B and specifically the heavy industrial market.

The Revenue Engine is more than just demand gen, lead gen, or pipeline management. It's a philosophical approach, a framework, supported with clear measurement principles that engage prospects before, during, and after their in-market motion through awareness, engagement, and customer acquisition.

At its core, the Revenue Engine framework is an easy-to-understand three-by-three matrix:

- Methodology: Share good news; track interest; follow up

- Funnels: The prospecting funnel, the nurture funnel, and the customer funnel

- Measurement: Volume, velocity, and value

THE REVENUE ENGINE FRAMEWORK
INCLUDES THREE ESSENTIAL PARTS

METHODOLOGY	FUNNELS	MEASURE
Share Good News	Prospect	Volume
Track Interest	Nurture	Velocity
Follow Up	Customer	Value

This book will provide a detailed, step-by-step plan or playbook you can apply to your revenue and growth efforts right now (or at least pretty darn soon). The key to our approach is that everything is underpinned by *real* measurement (more on real versus fake measurement later).

We'll show how great technology tools lead to real marketing math, which provides proof of return on investment. You'll find technology plays a big role in making B2B demand gen work today. We'll lay out a 101, 201, and 301 version of each. The goal is to just *get started* even if it's with a Scotch-taped tech stack.

We're going to talk a lot about math. Oh, and trust me, I get the people who break out in hives at the thought of math. Try to think of it as more Sherlock Holmes and less Einstein. It's about understanding the principles and interpreting the clues to develop a point of view. It isn't scary, I promise. And you'll be able to do it on the back of a napkin.

If the only marketing your company does is writing useless blog posts on a website no one visits, this book is for you because it's time to change that. If you've burned through a bunch of marketers because you've never seen the "value" in what they do all day, this book is for you. If you need someone to explain to you how to ask your marketer for real math and to show what good looks like, this book is for you.

And if you're a B2B marketer, this playbook is for you. If you are a "young me" who, like me, wants a road map for how to understand what's possible, and you really want to impress your boss (and maybe her boss), this book is for you.

You know there's more to your job than writing copy and sending emails. You crave a way to really build a funnel with proof of ROI. You are hungry for that executive leadership position. This book will help you get there.

If you want a seat at the table, welcome.

PART I

THE METHODOLOGY

If you had told me after that first executive leadership meeting that one day I would write a book about a successful, fully realized framework for demand gen that I created, I might have thought you were drinking some very special Kool-Aid. After all, you'll recall that I was woefully unprepared for what was going on and what was needed that day. I had no math and no plan at the table, but I did have the drive to participate and add value. And a killer PowerPoint presentation.

Since then, I've spent years perfecting a system that allows me and my team to deliver meaningful ROI-driven board-ready data for all types of B2B businesses. We've had incredible success and lots of failures along the way, all of which we've learned from. Like Oprah Winfrey says, "Failure is another steppingstone to greatness."

What we've learned on the road to creating the Revenue Engine framework:

1. Start with sharing your market-specific niche point of view.

2. Own all the records (email addresses) in your total addressable market and track the interest level of the content you're putting into the market.

3. Follow up. Fast. Often. Use different mediums.

4. Repeat.

WHAT DID WE LEARN?

1 Start with sharing your market-specific niche point of view.

2 Own all the records (email addresses) in your total addressable market, and track the interest level of the content you're putting into the market.

3 Follow up. Fast. Often. Use different mediums.

REPEAT REPEAT REPEAT

It sounds so simple, but most companies we engage with at Lead-Coverage, my consulting company, are doing one, maybe two of these well, and almost none are doing all three in a closed-loop repeatable process and measuring it all with a specific set of key performance indicators (KPIs) the C-suite has agreed will move the revenue needle.

You're not alone if this feels familiar. Latané Conant sees it in her CRO role at 6sense, a leader in intent data technology and a B2B GTM thought leader. She wrote *No Forms. No Spam. No Cold Calls: The Next Generation of Account-Based Sales and Marketing*, a text that has helped me immensely. "When revenue teams—and the people, processes, data, and tools involved in them—exist in silos, it's impossible to reach these modern buyers. Instead, sellers and marketers spin their wheels and have only false leads, long sales cycles, wasted time and resources, missed opportunities, inability to collaborate, and overall burnout to show for it."[5] Sound familiar? It is your job as a marketer to work with the revenue teams to locate and eliminate these disconnects. (Don't worry, *The Revenue Engine* has you covered.)

If it sounds too good to be true, let me assure you that it 100 percent is possible. I'm not saying any of this is easy, and it's definitely nuanced. But if you follow this framework, you will escape the trap of "random acts of marketing" (RAOM) and start to build a Revenue Engine that pumps out prospects ready to turn into customers. And you can do it right away.

Sangram Vajre and Eric Spett, in *ABM Is B2B: Why B2B Marketing and Sales Is Broken and How to Fix It,* say, "Winning in B2B is now a game of inches, not feet. It starts with effective, data-driven, dynamic targeting built on new types of account data that you can act on immediately, not tomorrow or next week."[6]

Now we are fortunate that we really can track account data—and use a framework that is measurable. My team and I have figured out what works *today.* Marketing has to change regularly—what works today won't work tomorrow. As you will see when we discuss artificial intelligence later in the book, with the advent of AI, what works today will be morphing into what works tomorrow.

It's important to always be measuring and iterating on what works. Professor John Dawes, Associate Director at the Ehrenberg-Bass Institute at the University of South Australia, created the Rule of 95, "95 percent of business clients are not in the market for many goods and services at any one time. Corporations change service providers such as their principal bank or law firm around once every five years on average. That means only 20 percent of business buyers are 'in the market' over the course of an entire year; something like 5 percent in a quarter—or put another way, 95 percent aren't in the market."[7]

This means we have to build a motion so when prospects are in market, they think of you. But ultimately the framework I am teaching you will help you not only market, but also find in-market signals and track that engagement.

True story: In 2013, I was the marketing consultant for one of the first digital freight brokers. Aaron Ross's *Predictable Revenue* had recently hit the market,[8] Outreach and Salesloft were new, and excitement was exploding around marketing technology. HubSpot was fairly nascent. Salesforce was definitely the dominant player, but it was really expensive and complicated. And so we were just testing approaches as much as we possibly could, which is very much what marketing does.

There were twenty-five sales reps on the floor (think *Wolf of Wall Street* style, minus the illegal activity), and I had eight reps on a desk who were testing my crazy marketing experiments. We were trying all sorts of approaches and measuring everything we could. Important to this book, this is where I really cut my teeth on how to measure what these people were doing out there in the sales and marketing trenches.

We were using a beta version of Outreach, which now has a valuation in the billions, through a tool called SendGrid, which allowed us to send eight hundred emails a night on behalf of each of our reps.

So I was writing these emails and sending them out on behalf of the reps every night. Then every morning they would come in, and they would have leads to respond to. In the very sexy realm of freight, we literally sent out an email saying, "Hey, I've got trucks in Arkansas, can I move a load for you?"

They were pretty innocuous emails, but every morning we would get responses. So they had about a 30-ish percent marketing qualified lead (MQL) rate, which was great (a little math there!). This happened for two or three weeks. Then over time I noticed that Sarah was getting four or five points higher MQLs than her male counterparts over the same time period. I remember feeling irritated because Sarah was not doing anything different.

In fact, *I* was the one writing all the content, sending the emails, and running the experiments. So the results should have been the same for everyone. The only thing that was different was Sarah's gender. I had a light bulb moment: Let's turn all the boys into girls. Bob became Rachel; Joe became Sheila. We had a whiteboard behind us with who's who, so in case Bob goes to the bathroom, Joe could answer Rachel's calls.

We got a 10 percent lift on our MQLs. Everybody was happy. We were doing a great job. The team was coming in every morning and replying to emails. It worked.

However, this gender-based difference was still amusing to me. One evening I met with a fellow marketer and relayed the remarkable uptick when we switched the gendered names the emails were from.

She asked who our target clients were, and I explained it was the male-dominated freight industry. So my clever friend asked, "Why don't you use even catchier names?" On a napkin, we came up with names like Bambi, Angel, and Sapphire. (With no offense intended to people with those names!)

With our new names, we leaped to a 98 percent email open rate and the highest MQL rate of the quarter.

Sex sells.

The actual point of this story is that you need to test—like a scientist—and keep adjusting one approach or another until you figure out what works. And to be honest, humorous but true story aside, figuring out what works is even *more* important today.

In Part I, we will explore in detail the three parts, or the "triple infinity," of the framework:

The triple infinity is the reminder that marketing is not an event, it's an ongoing process. The work of sharing good news, tracking the interest of the good news, and following up on those buying signals is never done.

B2C (business to consumer) big brands we know and love still advertise—Nike, McDonald's, Chick-fil-A, Coca-Cola. All these brands that have become household names don't treat marketing like a one-time event; the process of sharing their good news is never-ending. The same is true in B2B, but in my experience, B2B C-suite leaders don't see marketing as an "always on" engagement or a meaningful growth lever.

When a strong GTM motion is activated following this framework, the GTM team can follow prospects on their journey through our three funnels: prospect, nurture, customer. But the work is never done, The good news may change, the tracking signals and tools will be different, and the follow-ups will be done by different teams, but the work never stops.

We never stop executing against these three processes. We are always sharing good news, tracking the interest, and following up. If you stop the motion of these three activities, you're dead in the water. And the opposite of a strategic, repeatable approach to these tactics is the cardinal sin of GTM—RAOM.

We'll explore each of these steps in detail next:

- Chapter One: Share Good News

- Chapter Two: Track Interest

- Chapter Three: Follow-Up

One of the aspects of this book I am most passionate about is you can use the framework to put these powerful ideas into practice right now. I hope you have many "aha" moments as you read—whether you are a marketer, sales leader, or a CEO—and when you finish the book, I hope you have the tools to execute your own Revenue Engine.

CHAPTER 1

SHARE GOOD NEWS

GREAT CONTENT IS THE BEST WAY TO BUILD A LOYAL FOLLOWING. WHEN PEOPLE FIND CONTENT THAT THEY LOVE, THEY'LL COME BACK FOR MORE. AND THEY'LL TELL THEIR FRIENDS ABOUT IT TOO.

—SUSAN WOJCICKI, FORMER CEO OF YOUTUBE

When you think about the Revenue Engine framework, think three-by-three. There are three parts to the framework, with each of those also being comprised of three parts. The first part is the methodology. It's straightforward but highly effective. The methodology includes sharing relevant news with the target audience, tracking their interest, and following up with personalized communication that hits the mark every time. We've seen this approach act like a magnet for ideal customers, drawing them in and keeping their attention.

The next part of the framework is the three funnels. These funnels make this framework simple yet powerful. There're the prospecting funnel, the nurture funnel, and the customer funnel. Each one has a crucial role in turning prospects into customers for life.

The final part is measurement, and its three parts are volume, velocity, and value. The Revenue Engine's 3Vs of the B2B GTM measurement will allow you to measure, create reports for, and share the critical math around GTM activities.

THE REVENUE ENGINE FRAMEWORK
INCLUDES THREE ESSENTIAL PARTS

METHODOLOGY	FUNNELS	MEASURE
Share Good News	Prospect	Volume
Track Interest	Nurture	Velocity
Follow Up	Customer	Value

These elements all work together. We share news that drives interest in your ideal customer profile (ICP) that leads them to the prospecting funnel. As that prospect moves through your funnels, you collect buying signals, and they become a customer. We can mathematically measure the journey and deliver the math your leadership team is looking for. In Part III you will learn to measure the three Vs for your ROI "proof."

In this first chapter, we start with what is involved in sharing good news—a key part of the framework. I know what you're going to say. I've heard this before, depending on their industry: "I don't have PR 'good news' to share. We just _____." (Fill in the blank.)

You do have good news. It can be customer wins, partnerships, product launches, an analyst report, and the list goes on.

This chapter will explore:

- The required elements of good news: it must be relevant, timely, and market specific.

- The importance of a point of view in your good news.

- Why good news should be audience specific, and why you need to know your audience.

- The tracking and tying shared good news to revenue because we're all about the math.

- Building credibility for your good news through analyst relations and why it requires a strategic approach.

- The need to view trade shows and in-person events as more than just networking opportunities.

Let's start with understanding what good news is. And before you say it, yes, you do have good news to share.

WHAT IS GOOD NEWS?

Marketing agencies overcomplicate the content process with unnecessary jargon—content flywheel, branding, messaging, GTM, inbound—but it's all the same. It's good news shared with the *right audience*. So let's look at what good news actually is.

We'll keep it simple. Good news must have three elements:

1. Good news must be relevant and timely.

2. Good news must be market specific.

3. Good news has a point of view.

GOOD NEWS
MUST HAVE THREE ELEMENTS

1 Good news must be relevant (in other words: timely)

2 Good news must be market specific

3 The good news must have a specific point of view

Good news is anything that interests your target customer and can include the following:

CUSTOMER WINS	PARTNERSHIPS	PRODUCT LAUNCHES	ANALYST REPORTS (SUCH AS GARTNER, FORRESTER, FROST & SULLIVAN)
INDUSTRY RECOGNITION AND AWARDS	TRADE MAGAZINE BYLINES (YOU WRITE 600 TO 800 WORDS AND THEY PUBLISH IT)	A CUSTOMER CASE STUDY (SHOWING YOU SOLVED A PROBLEM FOR A LONG TIME CLIENT)	A PUBLICATION (BOOK OR ARTICLE)
FEATURE COVERAGE (FROM NATIONAL, TRADE, AND VERTICAL MEDIA)	EXECUTIVE THOUGHT LEADERSHIP ON LINKEDIN	TRADESHOW ACTIVITY	INDUSTRY-SPECIFIC DATA, FORECASTS AND ANALYSIS

Every company has good news.

As I wrote earlier, you may be thinking, "I have no good news to share. We just do what we do. Who cares about that?" I have news for you. You do have news, and your current customers as well as your potential customers care. Don't discount yourself, thinking, "Oh, we're just a ____ (enter company type here)." You are making a difference to your customers by solving their critical problems, and that's good news because it is valuable to *them*.

Good news cannot be you virtually patting yourself on the back (even if you deserve it). It must help the people you are trying to reach to see that you have the knowledge, skills, or product to improve their lives, and ideally that recognition comes from a respected third party. You must demonstrate value, and there's no better value endorsement than one bestowed by the market—an analyst, journalists, or your customers.

Remember, a key component of good news is it must be relevant to the people you are trying to reach. For example, you might be opening a new location for an important reason pertinent to your industry. You might be taking a contrary or disruptive position on something that's really interesting. The key is relevancy to your potential future customer's problems. Winning an award for best logo design is only good news for you. Helping a customer reduce downtime and the resulting impact on their bottom line is a win for them and good news to share.

One of my favorite books on content is Donald Miller's *Building a StoryBrand*. In it he goes into detail about how to make your customer the hero. Customer stories about how you helped them solve problems are the best news you can share. And as Latané Conant says, "Make sure you're the one they're learning from."[9]

It's your job as a marketer to help the customer understand that you not only understand their pain, but that you are also solving it in real ways that add real value to their businesses. That's good news.

Once you know your good news, and you have unified its messaging, you'll need to integrate that messaging across all channels. Conant calls it being a "category king," which I love. "Part of being a category king is conditioning the market to think like you. That starts with your own team and permeates out. So in building a unified message that embodies your sales narrative, you need to integrate the new messaging into every single marketing asset you have—each web page, LinkedIn profile, email communication, brochure—you get the idea."[10] To do this, you need the sales and marketing teams to be aligned—more on that later.

Announcing partnerships is another form of good news; plus, it lends you industry credibility. Partnership announcements are easy to execute and show alignment with another established company or strategy within a specific niche.

Partnerships can also be referred to as "category entry points," basically other brands that give your brand credibility. As the authors of *How Brands Grow* note, research suggests that strategic partnerships, relationships, or close associations will provide access to new category entry points (CEPs), expanding your brand's reach and awareness.[11] Credibility reduces risk to the buyer. Like the old saying, "No one gets fired for buying IBM." You want to de-risk the buying decision for your prospect.

Aside from partnerships, industry awards are another easy-to-execute strategy and can showcase a business case or customer win, which are all good news. You could consider recommending a customer for an existing award—potentially a customer you're looking to develop as an ongoing reference. In our industry there is the "Best Supply Chain Project of the Year." We nominate a customer or a prospective customer for awards like this. By nominating your customer, you make it about them, not you; your company is the facilitator, or the "guide." Sharing the good news about your partnership with the category leaders in your space is an easy way to start.

GOOD NEWS MUST BE RELEVANT AND TIMELY

Now you understand that yes, you do have good news to share. You know what to consider good news, and you know you'll need to amplify that good news across multiple channels. Remember that good news also must be relevant and timely.

Let's go back in time to March 2020 and the start of the pandemic. Suddenly the world was learning how the supply chain works, and the press wanted supply chain stories. LeadCoverage, my company, had the market covered.

Before the global COVID-19 pandemic, most companies had underinvested in supply chain resources and technology, and suddenly something that was invisible was now important.

Everyone will remember the rising cost of toilet paper as it all but disappeared from grocery store shelves during the early months of the pandemic, not to mention the "run" on alcohol-based hand sanitizer. No one, not the least of which the supply chain industry, was prepared for the sudden rise in demand due to everyone shopping from home and legitimately fearing for the future against a virus that no one fully understood. Until now the average person wasn't thinking about toilet paper inventory and how it gets moved from the manufacturer to the distributor to retailer to end user (pun intended).

With the spotlight completely on the process of "moving boxes" (our bread and butter), the supply chain industry soon saw an influx of private equity and venture capital investors suddenly interested in a $2 trillion market they had not explored to date.[12] Previously mundane, rote processes like ocean container visibility, warehouse distribution, lumper payments, and even drayage operations became inflection points in the health and success of the US economy, as well as immediate opportunities for investment and growth.

At the same time, there was a dearth of talent, a lack of great GTM B2B marketers, specifically heavy industrial B2B marketers. In general, people aren't going to Harvard B-school to go into the heavy industrial sector or freight brokerage. FinTech is sexy. MarTech is hot. Heavy industrial isn't (or so some people think). Transportation doesn't even make the list on Harvard Business School's employment and recruiting page.

That's where we came in. *This was our moment.*

Warehouses facing labor issues focused on worker safety became an interview with a warehouse robot company. Ocean containers were stuck on the wrong side of the globe, so we gave reporters the CEO of a company that had been moving containers for forty-five years. Ports across the country were experiencing historic delays and backlogs, and we gave reporters insight from a company that worked in every coastal and inland port in the United States. We gave them good news.

The point is, your potential customers want to hear about how you are solving the problems of the day, the issues that are top of mind when the news cycle is cresting. When you can hit that mark, you are sharing third-party-validated, relevant good news that can be repurposed and amplified in a demand generation program.

CASE STUDY

I will give you an example of relevant and timely good news in action with one of my clients, ITS Logistics. ITS is a leader in the supply chain execution and technology space, based in Reno, Nevada. During our intake due diligence, they shared that they operate at every coastal and inland port in the United States. The timing was just post-pandemic when there was a massive surge in import volumes coming into the US and consequently an increased focus on global import activity by C-suite leaders in the shipping community. This is a strategic advantage they hadn't found a way to tell their audience about—yet.

We worked with the ITS leadership team to execute and share the best data and good news we had and turned it into the ITS "Port Rail-Ramp Index." While it may not mean anything to you, for their specific ideal customer profile (ICP), this sort of valuable information was just what they were looking for to solve immediate problems. This unique, relevant, and timely good news is shared monthly and is now syndicated and frequently cited on CNBC, Reuters, and in key trade publications relevant to their desired Fortune 500 audience. That is very good news indeed. For everyone, including us.

GOOD NEWS MUST BE MARKET SPECIFIC

Being relevant isn't enough. Your good news needs to be market specific. Every industry has market jargon. Your ICP may or may not fit into one industry. If you sell fabrication services, you may be sending good news to auto companies, building materials manufacturers, or even subassembly companies. Each ICP will have words and acronyms that matter to them. As Donald Miller tells us, a good marketing message is one that "nobody has to burn calories to understand." In other words, talk to your ICP in the language that resonates with them.

Every ICP has goals, so use them to make your good news relevant. Adding this to a unique selling proposition that really connects to the audience will help your ICP engage with your content, leading to the buying signals you're looking for.

So what is an ICP? An ICP is a clear description of the ideal customer for your business—and we will learn how to create them in chapter two and also learn to have discipline and not chase fancy logos—but actual customer profiles that fit your business. A buying persona, on the other hand, adds depth regarding the individuals within that profile (like "Finance Frank" in chapter two's section: "ICP Versus TAM Versus Persona").

There can be many personas inside an ICP. The B2B buying committee is growing. According to Gartner, "The average enterprise B2B buying group consists of five to eleven stakeholders, who represent an average of five distinct business functions."[13]

Good news must be relevant to the people you are serving—and that requires intimacy. It requires you, as a marketer, to know what the people you are trying to reach need to hear or learn—*know* that ICP. And if you are a CEO or someone looking to hire a marketer, it requires finding someone who speaks to the people you are trying to reach with relevant good news in language and facts that mean something to them. You need to have a deep working knowledge about who your ICP is, what they care about, how they speak, what keeps them up at night, and how you solve their problems.

Sharing good news is step one for most of the companies we work with. Usually we're working on getting a regular, repeatable, and relevant public relations and content program off the ground. If you're already doing that, the next phase of sharing good news is adding personalization to your market-specific content. More on that in chapter ten on account-based marketing.

In a strong GTM motion, the *who* is more important than the *what*.

THE WHO IS MORE IMPORTANT THAN THE WHAT.

GOOD NEWS HAS A SPECIFIC POINT OF VIEW

Part of our framework is ensuring we take our time to discern our ICP, which we'll spend more time on in chapter three. For our purposes in this chapter, we'll consider who, specifically, we are trying to share good news with. You'll also need to thoughtfully determine who that good news is coming from and ensure it's something your audience can actually use.

To differentiate yourself and to be relevant to your ICP, you must have a point of view on something that is important to them. There is a big difference between advice and a point of view. For example, a blog post on "The Five Things to Consider When Choosing Your Transportation Management System (TMS)" doesn't share a point of view. It may offer salient advice, but sharing good news is more than sharing a feature set or throwing AI-based content onto a blog. (Spoiler alert: no one is reading your blog.) It is not sales copy. Good news with a point of view offers value and information. As Seth Godin says in *This Is Marketing: You Can't Be Seen until You Learn to See* that you have to stand for something. If you're a marketer, you're a leader in a company. The best thing you can do is have a point of view.[14]

Adding to that, the point of view needs to come from someone who is relevant to your ICP. We have a strategy at LeadCoverage that originally worked for us, and now we've turned it into a real strategy for our clients. We call it executive thought leadership, or ETL for short. The ETL comes from the leadership team. They tend to have the biggest reach on LinkedIn and usually have large followings after spending decades in the industry. Also, LinkedIn rewards human connections, so you have to be sure to share from the human, not the company. Which makes sense considering leaders usually have a strong audience who listens to them due to the very nature of their corporate roles. We can attribute more than $3 million in revenue to this strategy for our small business, so we put it to work for others.

We use the repeatable "share good news" motion we build with public relations, timely and specific content, and a point of view to power the incredible engine that is LinkedIn. Generally the C-suite of any company will have the biggest networks in your space because of tenure and relationships. LinkedIn, though, rewards human conversations, not corporate communications, so we share this timely, relevant content with a point of view from one *person's* LinkedIn account, then like, share, and engage to get the social media algorithm to work in our favor.

EXECUTIVE THOUGHT LEADERSHIP (ETL) TIPS:

1. Perfection is the enemy of progress. Post all the time on whatever is relevant.
2. LinkedIn rewards human interactions, so having a controversial point of view on a topic could be what you need to kick off a real conversation.
3. Less than 1 percent of your followers will see your content, so you have to share *much* more than you think you should.
4. Harnessing the power of LinkedIn for thought leadership *can* turn into a revenue-generating strategy, but connecting LinkedIn back to demand gen activities can be difficult. Our suggestion is tracking the logos of target accounts (more on that later).

This is a strategy we've seen work, but here's a stark truth. You can have twenty thousand LinkedIn followers and think whatever you put out there has a lot of reach. You may think you have a big network. You may have contributed toward the $3 million in revenue gained from ETL. But if you couple that with trade publications, it would literally be a game changer. Don't discount the trades. In our industry it's *Supply and Demand Chain Executive*, *Supply Chain Dive*, or *Inbound Logistics*, there is a list for your industry too. With their following, you are not even close to as powerful as the smallest trade publication in your space.

The power of the trades cannot be discounted in B2B demand gen. You must make friends with them. They're always looking for content and are the constant at all the trade shows where you'll be looking to make an impact. They're your panel hosts and your webinar moderators. Bring them in.

THE POWER OF COMMERCIAL PR

We love public relations firms; part of what LeadCoverage does is PR. But we think of it as "Commercial PR."

The difference is subtle but important when it comes to building a Revenue Engine. PR and Commercial PR focus on different strategies and measurement. Traditional PR is broader and focuses on reputation and relationships; Commercial PR is more targeted, with a strong emphasis on measurable outcomes and the strategic use of digital tools to achieve specific business goals.

PR aims to create a positive image and maintain a strong relationship with your audience. It's about your brand and can be measured through sentiment and social listening. Traditional PR encompasses a variety of activities like media relations, crisis communication, reputation management, and corporate communication.

Commercial PR focuses on measurable outcomes and data-driven strategies. The goal is to not just create a positive image or disseminate information, but to drive specific, measurable actions from the target audience. Commercial PR campaigns are part of the demand gen motion and are closely monitored for effectiveness.

Commercial PR is about using market-specific macro- and microeconomic news and turning it into content that your ICP wants to read. Whether that news is related to an economic index, COVID-19's implications on your industry, or a strike, it's your point of view on that topic that turns into demand gen content that drives revenue.

Note: It is possible to measure the ROI of public relations. But it's not easy.

Up next I've asked Will Haraway, chief content officer at Lead-Coverage, to provide his insights into analyst relations. Commercial PR and analyst relations are tied together in the way we go to market for our clients. In fact, sometimes we use analysts in our PR. Here's Will with a deeper dive.

ANALYST RELATIONS

SHARING GOOD NEWS WITH THE RIGHT WHO

CONTRIBUTION BY WILL HARAWAY, CHIEF CONTENT OFFICER AT LEADCOVERAGE

Analyst relations is the most mysterious of all the marketing disciplines and therefore my very favorite. It's equal parts discipline and organization combined with strategy, networking, and relationship building.

A quick primer: Analyst firms provide enterprise companies with the deep expertise and market research needed to help make multi-million-dollar capital investment decisions. Like any B2B industry, this is particularly important in logistics and supply chain, because many times pain points can be very specific based on your vertical industry. A warehouse management solution (WMS) specific to the food and beverage industry can be very different from a WMS for consumer goods retail, or pharmaceuticals, or automotive, and on and on and on. We joke that supply chain is just "moving boxes," but the metrics—speed, accuracy, efficiency—matter in different measures depending on what kind of boxes you are moving and what's inside them. The same goes with a transportation management solution (TMS), distributed order management (DOM), or supply chain planning (SCP). There are hundreds of permutations in every node of the supply chain, and every one of them has a universe of analysts attached providing enterprise-level research and influence.

For many, analyst firms begin and end with Gartner, and that makes sense—Gideon Gartner literally founded the modern analyst industry[15] and remains the leader. Countless multimillion-dollar decisions are made every year on the findings of their Magic Quadrants, Market Guides, and Hype Cycles.

If you are new to marketing and are unfamiliar with Gartner and/or analyst relations, you need to know that big enterprise companies like McDonald's, Walmart, or John Deere use the appropriate Gartner magic quadrant to inform their decision-making. Additionally, where Gartner puts you on a quadrant, if at all, matters because it means you will or won't get access to customers. This is serious business.

OWN YOUR NICHE AND DIVERSIFY YOUR ANALYST PORTFOLIO

There's no question that almost every analyst relations strategy needs to start with whether Gartner is actively planning research in your industry. But there are several strategic firms to work with—Forrester, Nucleus Research, Armstrong, IDC, Ventura, and Frost & Sullivan just to name a few. Gartner's research cycles are extensive, and specialized analyst firms can be flexible on coverage times and very specific to the strengths of technology in a particular industry. Its true end results are both the research notes and the conversations between lead analysts and end-user buyers that drive investment. The right conversation between a CEO/CIO and an analyst can lead to multiyear, multimillion-dollar buying decisions. In fact, Kara once had a supply chain professional tell her, "My prospects don't get out of bed without checking Gartner."

The value of that analyst coverage and positioning is a major part of a comprehensive demand generation strategy. The analyst coverage could be a market guide, a full magic quadrant, or just a report. You can even have smaller analyst firms write reports on your company. This third party gives you credibility to the marketplace. And it's what your buyer uses to build a case to their leadership team about which software to buy or vendor to choose, etc. Once published and licensed, this report should become the good news you share in the form of a press release, email campaign, and landing page. Good news backed with the highest level of expertise and credibility.

None of this, of course, happens overnight. You have to start by building your own analyst universe: every analyst and firm that could potentially have an opinion on your technology or service and where it fits within industries and verticals versus the competitors in your space. Gartner will take more of the macro view but won't generally address an industry space unless it is maturing and has a healthy number of competitors. If you are in a new or an emerging space, it could take several years for it to evolve from Cool Vendors to Market Guide to Magic Quadrant, and the gap between that definitive, vendor-centric research can be anywhere from twelve to eighteen months apart.

For many leadership teams, that lead time, expense, and "unmeasurable" effort is daunting when entering the analyst relations game. This effort is very hard to measure. This is where the strategic analyst firms are critical to your overall strategy.

Let's say for example that you're recognized as a Niche Player of the Magic Quadrant™ for Real-Time Transportation Visibility Platforms. Being recognized is a major accomplishment. It means that Gartner has delivered an honest assessment about your company to the marketplace.

You may encounter that your C-suite is underwhelmed by where Gartner chooses to position your company in a quadrant "niche," which can have a negative connotation to some, but we have a different point of view. This is your opportunity to *own* your niche.

Gartner's research in general is macro-inclined, meaning they cover so many sectors that it's impossible to go particularly deep. There are strategic analyst firms that specialize in going deep, and you can work with these firms to develop research that speaks directly to your specific niche. You can get into the minutiae of how your technology is specifically making an impact in your space and why and get specific customers involved as references.

Investing in analyst relations not only affects the diversity and breadth of coverage, but also the frequency. As opposed to elevating your analyst relations efforts once a year within your overall demand strategy, if strategized well, you can plan to have a report to share quarterly, providing your sales team with more highly credible touchpoints that could make the difference in closing more and faster. The more you understand the analyst firms, the more options you will identify and add to your overall marketing/demand generation plan and calendar.

NETWORKING IS KING

We all know that phrase, right? It's no different in analyst relations. No one is going to do it for you. The only way to find your specific analyst universe, where you can be the superhero, is to network the same way you would at a cocktail party. You start with the person you know or makes sense to approach, and you chat them up until you're introduced to someone else.

CASE STUDY

Starting in 2021, Redwood Logistics, a Chicago-based leader in third-party logistics (3PL) logistic execution and supply chain technology, doubled down on analyst relations as a GTM strategy. 3PL execution means that Redwood was moving freight on behalf of their customers. Companies like Apple or Kellogg's often outsource their shipping to a third-party logistics company. They may or may not have assets: trucks and warehouses.

Redwood had invested in becoming a technology company. The goal was to become not just a 3PL, a company that moves freight, but a technology company that helps their customers connect their whole supply chain and all their partners by a sophisticated technology. Some would call this a 4PL, or fourth-party logistics. Adding technology is the extra dimension and a radical shift for the company.

Part of the GTM plan involved working with Gartner to position their overall strategy as a 4PL, a new and emerging market for Gartner. Garter hadn't executed a 4PL study, so there was no report, market guide, or a magic quadrant on 4PL.

Redwood met with a dozen supply chain and 3PL Gartner analysts, month over month, until being introduced to the newly formed team managing the first ever 4PL market research. Replacing the existing 3PL Magic Quadrant, this team delivered a 4PL Innovation Insight report that evolved into a Market Guide for 4PLs the following year. Redwood's executive team worked with the Gartner team every step of the way to ensure the right reflection of the company within the research, which helped define their new company positioning as a modern 4PL. The twenty-three-year-old, 1.2-billion-dollar company orchestrates logistics execution and supply chain technology through an open-integration platform, showcasing their modern 4PL architecture.

This GTM positioning was directly influenced by the analyst relations strategy and provides valuable setting for Redwood's overall demand gen program.

TIMELINE

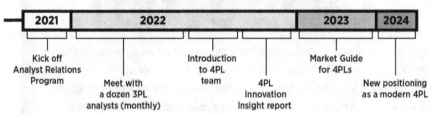

2021	2022	2023	2024

Kick off
Analyst Relations
Program

Meet with
a dozen 3PL
analysts (monthly)

Introduction
to 4PL
team

4PL
Innovation
Insight report

Market Guide
for 4PLs

New positioning
as a modern 4PL

THE VALUE OF ANALYST RELATIONS (AR)

Let's say your networking has paid off, and now you know who the right *who* is. Now it's time to show the value of AR to leadership, which can be challenging. We know it's an expensive proposition, from the multiple licenses to, ahem, engaging LeadCoverage (or a firm like ours) for strategy, and historically the ROI has been more than a little squishy. Why? The main return comes from enterprise-level deals and conversations that end-user execs have with key analysts under nondisclosure. If the analyst told vendor clients every time an enterprise executive was making a buying decision, they would just end up looking at RFPs all day. Sometimes, sure, an analyst will give you a hint that something is brewing, but for the most part, you don't know about those conversations until after the deal is signed.

Thus it can be a frustrating endeavor to keep tossing money at an AR program without understanding the ROI.

CREATING A CATEGORY

When what your company does doesn't fit nicely into an analyst "box," you have the opportunity to create a category. This is easier said than done and can take significant strategy and investment, but the payoffs can be enormous. It's our job to find the analysts that care about what's coming next so they can give a third-party view on the industry referenceable by buyers.

Such was the case with GreyOrange. They are a premier robot technology company and around 2020 took their GreyMatter platform to market. GreyMatter is a technology that "orchestrates" all the robots within the four walls of the warehouse. Along the way they added a key designation—GreyMatter is agnostic as to *what* robot it can orchestrate for a company, no matter the vendor. Now a shipper can use any robot company, working together in service of a shared customer.

We showed this platform to Gartner, with GreyOrange's Akash Gupta (cofounder, then CTO, now CEO) as the thought leader behind the concept. The robotics research team was intrigued, but there was no market for this category in 2021. Warehouse robotics as a whole was just about to explode almost entirely because of the safety and retail demand issues caused by the COVID-19 pandemic. We had created an emerging category, but it didn't have a name.

Gartner's lead analyst reached out and asked us to help name the new category. A real thrill. The team spent the next six weeks brainstorming category names like "Distributed Robot Fulfillment" and "Distributed Fulfillment Execution." We settled on "Multirobot Orchestration Platforms" and quickly changed it to "Multiagent Orchestration" to fit intelligent picking arms and doors, etc. under the umbrella.

And presto! A category—starting in 2022 you can find Multiagent Orchestration Platforms outlined and mentioned in twelve to fifteen different Gartner research notes every year, a staple in Execution Hype Cycles and the Warehouse Magic Quadrant with a growing list of vendors in the space.

Most importantly, GreyOrange had validation for their innovation and a launchpad for GreyMatter sales just as the Warehouse Robotic market was reaching its peak post-pandemic.

THE POWER OF ANALYST RELATIONS

CASE STUDY

Gartner isn't the only analyst name in the game; smart AR strategists will use that to your advantage. We will use GreyOrange as an example. While the company has started to find its way with Gartner coverage post-pandemic, it was mostly downstream and couched within warehouse management software and automation research.

A smaller but well-run analyst firm out of India, Quadrant Knowledge Solutions, started covering the autonomous mobile robots (AMR) space, and lo and behold their research showed GreyOrange as the leader. Quadrant Knowledge is growing in reach year over year, but they would never claim to have the same reach as a Gartner or a Forrester. Still a leader is a leader, and their report was the only game in town regarding AMRs. So we built an entire program enhancing and maximizing the impact of this leadership position.

We shared this good news via PR, tracked interest via HubSpot landing pages, and followed up on the buying signals. This program resulted in:
- more than six hundred engaged contacts,
- fifty-nine form fills,
- and thirty-three net new leads in the funnel,
- and it's the thirty-three net new leads that were significant.

These buyers were drawn by the content and entered GreyOrange's funnel organically, meaning that other competitors wouldn't have them on their list. GreyOrange got the first crack at these thirty-three leads because of the content showing them in a clear leadership position in their space.

Just like that, real ROI that justifies the activity and the program. We all know AR has real value; the trick is showing it.

CONVERSATIONS WITH THE ENTERPRISE

Perhaps more than any other reason, the value of AR is in the relationship to the enterprise space. In this case, our definition of enterprise is a company with a market cap of $1 billion or more. When an enterprise looks to make a supply chain technology decision, analyst interactions, one-to-one relationships, and research will always be part of the decision-making process.

When your company commits to the AR process, it provides the discipline and language of presenting to the enterprise audience. What could be more valuable to your company's brand? Committing to a strategy, choosing a narrative, defining roles—these are characteristics that will benefit your company far beyond any specific research note. Understanding the content and strategy that will trigger buying decisions is a skill that will permeate throughout your organization, whether or not you put the content strategy I've laid out above into place and will raise the profile of everyone who participates in an AR program. But if you do, you'll be unstoppable.

TRADE SHOWS AND CONFERENCES: GOOD NEWS INCLUDES REAL HUMANS

One of the important ways people in B2B connect with potential new business—and share good news with—is through trade shows and conferences. After all, humans buy your products, and meeting them where they gather is a great strategy.

There are specific strategies for tracking the value of a trade show that we will share later. I know enterprises that spend millions of dollars on trade shows each year. Yet their marketing teams are not actually tracking attribution back to those trade shows. In fact, probably 99 percent of the people I talk to do not track shows at all. That's essentially spending a quarter of a million dollars or more and having nothing to show for it other than trade show booth swag and sore feet from walking the floor.

Conferences are an opportunity for marketing to flex its power and show what can be done. The branding marketers are saying, "Our booth looked good. We had great handouts, sharing good news with exactly the people we needed to reach. We had excellent traffic." (But no math!) Instead the conversation should be: "Let me tell you all the people that we brought to the booth. Let me show you all the humans we put in the CRM system. Let me show you all this math."

It pains me when marketers don't take advantage of opportunities to shine. Trade shows should be a GTM professional's personal playground. It is an ICP rich environment and prospects are walking by booths, attending speaking sessions, eating lunch, having cocktails. There are opportunities for paid media and to get in front of the press (especially trade press). There are even analysts who attend.

Trade shows are not only a chance to shine with those real, live humans you need to reach, they are also a chance for marketing to shine to the executive leadership team. Here they can do things that matter to the executive leadership team and to the board.

Instead what I see often is the misplacement on the measurement of trade shows. We'll hear contextually how well shows are going, but CEOs are going to ask for proof of ROI, and marketers rarely can share the actual math behind it (math I am going to teach you in this book!).

TRADE SHOW SCIENCE

TOTAL ATTENDEES
TOTAL TAM ACCOUNTS (OUR TARGETS)
OF PRE-SET MEETINGS WITH TARGETS
OF NEW BUSINESS CARDS COLLECTED
OF NEW LOGO OPPORTUNITIES

AND

OF PRESS INTERVIEWS
OF CURRENT CUSTOMER INTERACTIONS

$$\frac{\text{\# OF NEW OPPORTUNITIES}}{\text{ARR PER OPPORTUNITY}} + \text{VALUE OF PRESS OPPORTUNITIES} + \frac{\text{VALUE OF CURRENT CUSTOMER}}{\text{\# OF INTERACTIONS}} = \text{TRADE SHOW ROI}$$

SIMPLE TRADE SHOW ROI

$$\frac{\text{\# OF NEW OPPORTUNITIES}}{\text{OPENED AT EACH TRADE SHOW}} \times \text{ARR} = \frac{\text{SIMPLE}}{\text{TRADE SHOW ROI}}$$

REVENUE ENGINE RECAP

The first part of our Revenue Engine framework is share good news. There's an old motivational sales saying of "Always Be Closing." For marketers, I'd say, "Always Be Sharing" (good news).

There are several good news elements to keep in mind:

- Good news should be timely (old news is no news).

- Good news should be relevant to your potential customers— it must be market specific.

- Good news must have a point of view.

- AR is very important, especially when targeting enterprise prospects.

- Good news is meant to be shared with real, live people.

- Trade shows, especially in certain industries like supply chain, are fertile ground for networking.

- Good news must be tracked because remember, we're all about the math.

One more comment on sharing good news: it's a process that never stops. Good news will need to be shared on a regular basis, well, forever. To avoid the dreaded RAOM trap, use your trade show, public relations, and partnership calendars to drive timely demand gen campaigns. We recommend planning at least a quarter at a time and following the 80/20 rule.

The 80/20 rule is that content should be 80 percent evergreen or able to be sent at any time. It is pain-point and value-proposition specific, oftentimes seasonal and maybe even announcement dependent. Twenty percent of your content should be event driven and based on news happening in your industry. In supply chain, it can be weather, port congestion, mergers and acquisitions, labor strikes, or bankruptcies. Use these market-specific events to drive 20 percent of your content and hit when the iron is hot.

Sharing your good news is only the beginning. You've got to track the interest of your ideal customers on your good news. In other words, you need to gather buying signals, and in today's digital world, that's easier to do than ever before.

The first step in our hierarchy is done. You're ready to share good news. And we're going to cover tracking the interest on that good news in our next chapter.

CHAPTER 2

TRACK INTEREST

EXECUTIVES HATE TO DO THIS BECAUSE THEY FEEL THEY ARE SHRINKING THEIR MARKET OPPORTUNITY, BUT THE WISDOM SAYS, "PICK A NICHE, GET RICH."

—**AARON ROSS**, *PREDICTABLE REVENUE*

The road to revenue is paved with buying signals. They're the subtle (and sometimes not-so-subtle) cues that indicate someone is interested in what you have to offer. And thanks to the increasing accessibility of sales and marketing technology tools like HubSpot, ActiveCampaign, and Zoho, even the least-sophisticated GTM organizations can track the most fundamental buying signals—email responses and website visits. With them, you can peek into your future customer's behavior.

Before we dive into the specifics of tracking interest, let's take a moment to revisit the Revenue Engine framework's three interconnected elements: methodology (sharing good news, tracking interest, and following up), funnels (prospecting, nurture, and customer), and measurement (volume, velocity, and value). These components work together seamlessly to propel your business forward.

In the previous chapter, we explored how sharing good news that resonates with your ideal customer is the catalyst for drawing them into your prospecting funnel. As they progress through the funnels, you'll gather valuable buying signals that indicate their level of interest. Before long they'll transition from prospect to customer.

This chapter is dedicated to the critical task of effectively tracking interest. In it, we'll:

- Explore why understanding your total addressable market (TAM) is essential for navigating your revenue journey with clarity and precision.

- Learn how to identify and claim your ideal customer profile as your own, ensuring that you're targeting the right people with your efforts.

- Emphasize the importance of connecting with genuine, living, breathing individuals who have a real need for your product or service. It's not just about casting a wide net; it's about targeting those who are most likely to benefit from what you offer.

- Discuss why list hygiene is a crucial, ongoing aspect of the Revenue Engine framework. Just like maintaining good personal hygiene, keeping your lists clean and up to date is essential for the health and effectiveness of your marketing efforts.

- Cover informed decision-making when constructing your marketing technology (MarTech) stack. Selecting the right tools is like equipping yourself with a powerful arsenal that will help you track, analyze, and act upon buying signals with ease.

- Delve into the art and science of tracking buying interest and signals. It's a bit like being a detective, piecing together clues to form a complete picture of your customer's journey.

- Demonstrate the ROI of your efforts with clarity and confidence with the help of lead scoring and account dossiers.

- Ready to rev the engine?

THE WHO VERSUS THE WHAT

The question we ask every B2B GTM team we connect with is very simple but often hard for them to answer: "Do you own the email address of every human who could buy from you?"

Nine times out of ten, the answer is no.

Here's the hard truth. You can't track buying signals against a human you don't know exists. You must own an email address in your customer relationship management (CRM) tool before you can track that person's activity.

Also keep in mind that, according to Latané Conant, the 6sense CRO who wrote *No Forms, No Spam, No Cold Calls*, "the average buying committee at an enterprise is seven to nineteen people."[16] And yes, you should try to own all those email addresses.

Tracking is easier said than done for most B2B companies. In 2021 we started working with a freight bill pay and audit company. They work with some of the biggest international freight forwarders and freight brokers in the industry to make sure the millions of payments that are in the global supply chain are all correct. They operate teams all over the world, managing and tracking invoices for some of the biggest global brands we all know and love.

When we started our engagement, there was a moment of confusion on our end—they had just started a marketing function in full force, and they were using HubSpot, the right CRM for their level of sophistication. They had a few folks in their marketing group, including a leader and an account-based marketing specialist.

One of the first questions we asked was "How many records are there in your CRM?" And we didn't get a real answer. It was a little weird.

What we uncovered was though the total addressable market (TAM) was close to forty thousand companies, they had acquired only 2,500 email addresses. Yup, that's only 6 percent of their TAM.

This company could have produced the best marketing campaign ever executed, and it wouldn't have moved the needle. They were only reaching a sliver of their TAM.

The *who* you are marketing to is more important than the *what* you are marketing.

A NOTE ON *TAM*

In general use, TAM refers to the maximum amount of revenue a business can generate by selling their products or services in a specific market. Calculating TAM usually involves assessing the broader market for a product or service.

TAM is sometimes presented alongside serviceable available market (SAM), or the portion of the TAM targeted by your products and services within your geographical reach. Serviceable obtainable market (SOM) is the portion of SAM that you can capture.

We're keeping our Revenue Engine simple—for our purposes TAM is the number of companies who could potentially buy your product or service. Nothing fancy, no regression analysis or market assessment—a simple number. TAM should represent the goal for the number of companies and contacts that should be in your CRM.

OWN AND UNDERSTAND YOUR TAM

The first step in tracking interest is owning your TAM. Logic says you can't market to 6 percent of your total market and hit a *single* sales and marketing goal.

By this point in the book, I've impressed upon you that math is your friend. It is your friend not only because it will give you insights on the impact of your marketing efforts, but because math is the god(dess) of the boardroom (well, math that drives revenue).

So you've shared good news. You've followed framework step one and reached out to analysts, you've gotten some great placements in the media, and you've made a splash at a trade show. You're excited! Now what?

The next question the CEO or board is going to ask is, "Thanks so much for sharing all that good news. We really appreciate the *New York Times* profile, the CNBC screen time, and the earned media trade bylines, but did it lead to revenue? Did it actually contribute to our desired growth?"

You may think I'm joking, but this is a real conversation I've heard as an employee and as a consultant. If you can't answer the ROI question, whatever you say next is irrelevant. You will be relegated to the "marketing" box and never invited back to the boardroom. Hello, "marketing girl."

If you want a seat at that table, if you want to be in the room where the action happens, you need to bring the math that shows that you are part of that decision-making process. You have to show that the good news you've shared has reached your target ICP. You have to prove that the right prospects have become aware of your company, and they may even have some interest in your value proposition.

Sounds like a lot? It is. But with the right tech stack and strategy, you can show the actual ROI of the good news and how it's driving pipeline or landed revenue, which is what we'll discuss in this chapter.

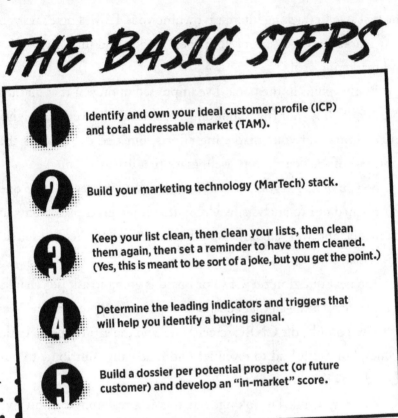

THE BASIC STEPS

1 Identify and own your ideal customer profile (ICP) and total addressable market (TAM).

2 Build your marketing technology (MarTech) stack.

3 Keep your list clean, then clean your lists, then clean them again, then set a reminder to have them cleaned. (Yes, this is meant to be sort of a joke, but you get the point.)

4 Determine the leading indicators and triggers that will help you identify a buying signal.

5 Build a dossier per potential prospect (or future customer) and develop an "in-market" score.

The steps to track interest are basic:

1. Identify and own your ideal customer profile (ICP) and total addressable market (TAM).

2. Build your marketing technology (MarTech) stack.

3. Keep your lists clean, then clean your lists, then clean them again, then set a reminder to have them cleaned. (Yes, this is meant to be sort of a joke, but you get the point.)

4. Determine the leading indicators and triggers that will help you identify a buying signal.

5. Build a dossier per potential prospect (or future customer) and develop an "in-market" score.

Let's look at the moving parts of this framework.

THE 4 OR 5 MAIN PARTS OF AN *ICP*

Ideal Customer Profile

FIRMOGRAPHIC INFORMATION

TECHNOGRAPHIC DATA

NEEDS AND PAIN POINTS

REGULATORY COMPLIANCE AND RISK PROFILE

GROWTH AND STABILITY (OPTIONAL)

IDENTIFY YOUR IDEAL CUSTOMER PROFILE (ICP)

Give significant thought and planning to who your ideal customer is and then create a profile. The good news is, unlike B2C, your ideal customer is probably not "every single human in the world who drinks soda." It's a lot more specific. The more specific, the better in GTM motions.

An ICP is the *company*, and it has company characteristics. *Personas* are humans who have roles on the buying committee and work for the ICP. According to Gartner, "The typical buying group for a complex B2B solution involves six to ten decision makers, each armed with four or five pieces of information they have gathered independently and must de-conflict with the group."[17]

Determining an ICP in a B2B GTM strategy involves a detailed analysis of your best existing customers and the market. The ICP helps you understand who your product or service is best suited for, enabling more focused and effective marketing, sales, and product development efforts.

There is a simple system for creating your ICP:

1. Analyze your current customer base. Starting with your most successful and satisfied customers, look for common characteristics. Look for commonalities like industry, company size, location, annual revenue, etc.

2. Make a list of your current customer's pain points and needs. Identify the specific challenges and problems that your product or service solves for these customers. Even better, identify the value proposition your company delivered that helped this customer choose your product/service over competitors.

3. Decide on clear firmographic and demographic criteria and don't change it. Making a decision on your ICP's company size, industry, verticals served, geographic location, and annual revenue, and sticking to it is just as important as any other decision you'll make in a GTM function.

4. Technographics can be very important, and they can give you a clear idea of the sophistication of an organization. Identify the technologies your ideal customers use today and how your product/service fits into that stack. Tools like BuiltWith

and SalesIntel can help you identify some of the tech stack your ICP is using today.

Ensure marketing, sales, product development, and customer service teams all understand and agree on the ICP. This alignment is critical for a cohesive GTM strategy.

IDEAL CUSTOMER
PROFILE SAMPLE

DEMOGRAPHIC DATA

Industry: CPG, Retail

Size: Enterprise

Revenue: $1 Billion+

Number of Employees: 5,000+

Customers Served: B2C, B2B, Retail

Type of Financing: Private Equity Owned or Public

Owned Manufacturing: Yes

Owned Fleet: Yes

Distribution Complexity: High

TECHNOGRAPHIC DATA

Current ERP: SAP or Oracle

Current WMS: Softeon or Similar

Current TMS: Manhattan or Similar

Current Sophistication: Med-High

Current Visibility Tool: project44 or FourKites

Conant writes: "When everything you do is derived from your ICP, it's like having guardrails in bowling; it's impossible to throw a gutter ball."[18]

Creating an ICP requires teamwork and leadership, and it's an ongoing process. Review your ICP quarterly as markets evolve, customer needs adjust, and your product or service develops. The better you understand your ICP, the more effectively you can tailor your GTM strategies to meet the needs of your most valuable prospects.

When you revisit your ICP as part of this ongoing review, you need to sit down, and ask, "Has our ideal customer changed?" The other question we often ask our clients is: "Is this your actual ICP, or is this your wishful thinking ICP?"

There is a big difference between "We currently service customers that are under a billion dollars in revenue" and "We would like customers over $10 billion in revenue, but we don't actually service them today." Those are two very different ICPs. You really need to decide, and it's a strategic decision by the business: Are we going to work on procuring customers that we currently have and replicate what we know we can do really well? Or are we really trying to go up or down market, which means we need to identify the next set of customers?

What's more important than a company that *is* your ICP? A clear picture of who is *not* an ICP.

Disqualification is just as important as a list of target accounts in a strong Revenue Engine. There's no use putting gas in the tank if it's the wrong kind. Cut your losses on "wish list" deals that are outside your clearly defined ICP and double down on those you can serve.

DEFINE YOUR TOTAL ADDRESSABLE MARKET (TAM)

Now you have locked in your ICP, your leadership team has given you the green light to move forward, and the sales team is excited about this new, clear direction.

Before you can track interest against these ICPs, you need to know the size of your market and acquire the email addresses of the people you're selling to.

Understanding the TAM is crucial for setting realistic sales goals, attracting investors, and making strategic business decisions. This is a great exercise to do with your sales leader partners. It's likely they've executed a similar exercise, and you two should be on the same page.

Because our definition of TAM is simple—just the number of companies that fit your identified ICP criteria—finding these companies *should* be relatively simple.

You'll need to choose a data technology partner for this. There are plenty to choose from: SalesIntel (our preferred tool), ZoomInfo, Dun & Bradstreet (for my boomers out there), Apollo, and the list goes on. You can also create your own database using multiple tools cobbled together.

Simply put your ICP characteristics into the data tool and see what it gives you in return. It won't be perfect but spend a day with it. Change the criteria, open the aperture, and see what happens when you go up and down market. This may impact the feedback you give to the GTM team on the ICP they decided on. It might be too limiting.

As of the writing of this book in 2024, there are 19,677 shippers with more than $100 million in top-line revenue in the United States. If we take the very basic math that the average company spends

7 percent of their top-line revenue on shipping, or $7 million in shipping, that gives us a pretty simple math to start with.

Then we break down those lists into industries, verticals, modes, tech stacks, warehouse square footage, etc. Your list of criteria could be endless.

Once you have come to a conclusion on the TAM, then you need to acquire the actual list of companies and contacts inside the TAM you've identified. (It can't be all fun consulting and framework building.)

If the average buying committee size is ten to fourteen people (I've shared there are many sources that agree this committee is growing and changing; the specific number and source are sort of irrelevant at this point), then to capture the top of the shipping market in the case study I've provided, you'll need the twenty thousand companies multiplied by ten people per company. That's two hundred thousand email addresses. That's a lot of email addresses.

Hence the question we always start with when we begin a GTM engagement: "Do you own the email address of every human who could be a customer?" If the answer is no, then the next question is "Do you know the number of companies in your TAM?"

The bottom line is you have to *own* the data you're pulling into your database, preferably a customer relationship management software (CRM), and pay attention to the value of the data, how you are sourcing it, and how often it is cleaned. Next we'll cover specific steps of list hygiene, which is incredibly important.

LIST HYGIENE: THE REVENUE ENGINE RULES FOR LIST CLEANING

Let's be honest. Not everything in your closet fits or is still on trend. Imagine you have a closet stuffed with clothes that are too big or too small, that fit better in 1998 than they do now, and look like they still belong in 1998. Now add some cords from computers you no longer own or that no longer work. Throw in a few music CDs and an old DVD or two. Now you have a packed closet filled with useless things that provide zero value.

WELCOME TO A DIRTY LIST: TIME TO GET CLEANING.

I have developed my own list-cleaning best practices. This is a bit detailed, but it will prove invaluable if you are a newer marketer and will give experienced marketers some ideas to consider. Follow these rules, rinse, and repeat.

1. Pull list of contacts from HubSpot/Salesforce into Excel.

2. Do your due diligence. De-dupe based on email addresses, update titles and naming conventions to be consistent (remove all caps, standardize job titles, etc.), make sure first name and last name are separate columns, and remove spam-type catchall emails like admin@, ap@, etc.

3. Bulk-verify existing data with a tool like BriteVerify or NeverBounce.

4. Remove any emails that come back invalid, unknown, or accept all. If using ZoomInfo or SalesIntel, send your list of "risky" data back to receive new data/credits.

5. Prepare your list for import. Tag the list appropriately in HubSpot so it is clear it is cleaned and ready for use. Add Lead Source and Lead Source Detail for list imports. Click "APPEND" not "REPLACE."

6. Use your list and monitor results. HubSpot/Salesforce will automatically suppress any unsubscribes, bounces, or spam alerts.

Note: Never delete a record from your CRM. Even if it's considered "dirty" or not useful or the human behind the record has unsubscribed. A record that's been deleted *can* be added again. Instead, suppress records no longer useful to you so they can't be added again and are not actively marketed to.

A NOTE ON *THE WORD "LEADS"*

Before we go any further, it's time for a quick word on the word "leads." We will cover this more in detail in the chapters on funnels in Part II. However, if you have spent time identifying your TAM, bought a bunch of names and emails from ZoomInfo or SalesIntel, they are not leads.

They are *records*.

A record is simply a name and an email address. They may work for a company that's in your TAM, but the human has not been identified as real. We haven't checked to see if the email address is any good. We don't know if they have a title that makes sense for us to market to—our *personas*. A record you download from a database represents nothing more than a record in your CRM. Don't give them any more credit than they deserve. And don't *ever* call them "leads" to senior leadership.

Why?

I'll tell you.

"Leads" are prospects that may close. They represent revenue to a c-suite executive. The word "lead" is a "leading" word (see what I did there?). It gives 100 percent the wrong impression to your leadership team. Until you know more information about this person, their role, the company, etc., they have *no value*. Using the word "lead" gives them value they haven't earned.

Records become leads or prospects when they have given at least one buying signal, which you will be tracking. That signal lets us know they're alive (the bare minimum). My advice is don't think about these email addresses as humans. They're not humans. They *represent* humans, but they're not humans until you actually send them an email, and you know (because someone actually reacts and also that it doesn't bounce back) there's a human being behind that email address.

I often use my mother-in-law as an example. She's a lovely lady. But if you put out the best gosh-darn press release about your new product feature that helps freight brokers move freight faster, and my mother-in-law sees it, it won't help you much. My husband's mom is a lovely woman, but she's not buying transportation management software.

OK, off my soapbox now and back to work.

ICP VERSUS TAM VERSUS PERSONA

If the ICP is a list of characteristics of the *perfect* customer, and the TAM is how many of those customers exist, then the personas are the humans inside those companies who work on the buying committee that will determine your fate. This is why it's extremely important to have these records in your database beyond having a contact email address for them. It's about understanding who they are inside their organization.

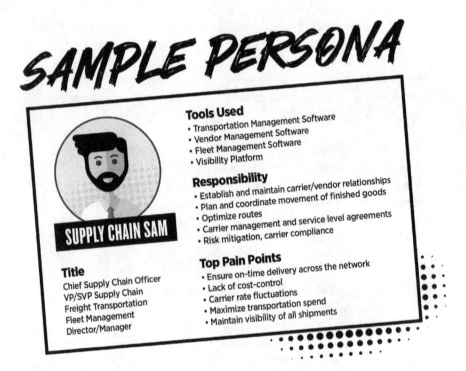

By definition, a persona is an archetypal representation of an existing subset of people who share similar needs, expectations, behaviors, and motivations. Personas are powerful tools for marketing and customer-experience planning, as they offer insight into what customers want and how they will engage.[19]

At LeadCoverage, we often create detailed psychographic profiles like "Finance Frank" and "Innovator Irene."

"Finance Frank"—Values transparency and efficiency, aims to reduce operational costs, is cautious about new technology, prioritizes ROI in decision-making.

"Innovator Irene"—Believes in leveraging cutting-edge technology, seeks solutions that drive competitive advantage, is open to taking calculated risks, focuses on long-term strategic benefits.

Using psychographic insights like these, you can tailor your messages and sales approaches based on their job title and goals. For instance, content for "Finance Frank" might focus on cost-benefit analyses, while "Innovator Irene" might be more interested in case studies showcasing innovation and long-term growth.

QUICK TIP

There are some super-creepy and sexy AI tools that help with psychographic profiling. More in Chapter 10, but my favorite is Crystal Knows. It can show you the DISC personality profile of anyone on LinkedIn before you even start a conversation. It's a powerful tool for sending the right kind of message to a specific type of person.

For example, I'm a "captain" and I abhor email. So if you want your email read, keep it short, and I love to learn about new stuff on the fly. My husband is an engineer by trade and a "skeptic." Since he doesn't like surprises, I send him all the details before a call so he can be prepared and to keep him engaged. Yes, you can know all this about strangers—before you ever meet.

Personas help with a targeted or an account-based marketing (ABM) selling strategy where you have identified a certain number of companies and the records that work there. Yes, they are still records because you are not sure who they are yet. You might think the email you have of Marge in accounting is the buyer of the type of software as a service (SaaS) you are selling. However, it could be that Marge has moved into human resources and has no need of your software. So when Marge gets your email, she presses delete. And does the same for your follow-up email. Marge is just a record until you know she is an actual human who can *buy* from you.

As Latané Conant says, ABM offers sales "a select list of the accounts most likely to convert to an opportunity, so [they] can take the time to get to know them and work them with highly personalized, multichannel, multipersona outreach."[20] That personalized multichannel outreach is empowered by technology, marketing technology or a MarTech stack. More on ABM later.

THE MARTECH STACK

The most important decision you can make as a marketer, marketing leader, or business leader responsible for GTM is the MarTech stack. The right technology stack for your industry, size, sophistication, and sales team can make or break your ability to execute campaigns, track ROI, and measure your successes. The wrong stack will set you back quarters or even years.

We had a venture capital (VC)-backed small business client at one point. For some reason, the VC pushed the CEO to buy Salesforce and Pardot as his CRM and marketing automation stack. We spent three times the amount of time and money managing an inflated tech stack he wasn't ready for. If he had a simpler stack, like HubSpot, ActiveCampaign, or even MailChimp, he would have been aligned with his level of sophistication (read: one marketer) and probably more successful. That's why it's critical that you don't just have a MarTech stack. You need to have the *right MarTech stack for you and your business.*

The right tech in the right place will identify whether your potential customers are interested in the news you're sharing. HubSpot is my favorite platform that allows even small companies to track interest and responses. Obviously large companies with large budgets can get more sophisticated, enterprise software that is customized. Ideally this sort of tech will increase click-through and conversion rates, react to consumer interest in real time, automate the customer journey, offer personalization, and so on.

The more sophisticated the tech stack, the more granular you can be about showing attribution or how your prospects come into your funnel in the first place. Attribution is hard and a skill that requires a strong stack and a skilled GTM team to manage well.

TRACKING INTEREST IN YOUR MARTECH STACK

We've discussed your ICP, TAM, and personas. Now let's dive into how you can effectively track interest in your MarTech stack.

The most crucial step in this process is ensuring you add the email addresses and record of someone who can buy from you into your CRM. By doing so you can then track their interactions with your brand across various touchpoints, such as landing pages, emails, webinars, and trade shows. This comprehensive tracking allows you to gain valuable insights into their level of interest and engagement. *So tracking interest is about owning your TAM.* You identify all the people who could potentially be a customer, and then you send them the good news that we talked about in chapter one.

But how do you know what MarTech stack is right for you? With the rapid evolution of marketing technology and the overwhelming number of options available, selecting the right MarTech stack can be intensely confusing. Scott Brinker has been tracking the number of marketing technologies since 2011 at ChiefMarTec. According to his research, there are now more than eight thousand different marketing technologies, valued at over \$120 billion.[21]

Clearly no one company is going to use eight thousand pieces of technology. So we've categorized MarTech stacks into three levels of sophistication: 101, 201, and 301. Identify which level best suits your needs and you can make an informed—and streamlined—decision.

The average B2B MarTech stack is between six and twenty different pieces of technology.[22] This is the highest-level view of the five main pillars of a MarTech stack. The list of options is endless.

MARKETING ATTRIBUTION JOURNEY

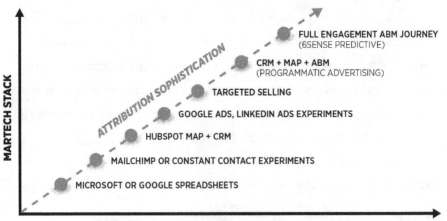

- FULL ENGAGEMENT ABM JOURNEY (6SENSE PREDICTIVE)
- CRM + MAP + ABM (PROGRAMMATIC ADVERTISING)
- TARGETED SELLING
- GOOGLE ADS, LINKEDIN ADS EXPERIMENTS
- HUBSPOT MAP + CRM
- MAILCHIMP OR CONSTANT CONTACT EXPERIMENTS
- MICROSOFT OR GOOGLE SPREADSHEETS

MARTECH STACK

ATTRIBUTION SOPHISTICATION

MATURITY OF REVENUE ATTRIBUTION TRACKING

MARTECH 101, 201, 301

	Data Source for List Building and TAM Analysis	Marketing Automation Platform (MAP)	Customer Relationship Management (CRM)	Buying Signal Activity Tracking	Intent
101	Leadfeeder or Apollo	MailChimp or Constant Contact	Spreadsheets, Google Drive, Pipedrive or Zoho	Google Analytics	Bombora
201	SalesIntel or ZoomInfo	HubSpot	HubSpot	Google + HubSpot	Rollworks or Terminus
301	SalesIntel	HubSpot or Marketo	HubSpot or Salesforce	Google Tag Manager + HubSpot	6Sense ABM

BUYING SIGNALS

The road to revenue is paved with buying signals. As you track interest in your MarTech stack, you'll begin to notice certain behaviors that indicate a readiness to buy. Those who are interested in your good news will start to send up these "buying signals." Some common buying signals include:

- Opening emails

- Replying to emails or invitations

- Signing up for webinars

- Visiting your website

Those are the little breadcrumbs that you need in order to turn those humans into actual customers. You and the sales team will determine which buying signals are most important to you and your business. Once you've identified and tracked these signals, those humans are not total strangers any longer. (And we will talk about strangers and prospects in chapter three.)

LIST HYGIENE IS ESSENTIAL TO YOUR SUCCESS—AND YOUR JOB

While it may not be the most glamorous aspect of marketing, list management is essential to the success of your campaigns. You'll need to get used to the idea that you need to spend a shocking amount of time managing lists, including:

- TAM and ICP lists

- Records from trade shows

- Partner and referral source lists

- Records from data sources

- Records from friendly, noncompetitive companies

Depending on your sector and specialty, you will have other lists. I realize list management is likely the last thing anyone wants to do. But I promise you, if you do not have list governance and proper list hygiene, your efforts to track activity and engage people may be wasted. All the energy and work that you are going to put into being able to track activity means you've got to be able to send your good news to people that actually want to get that message.

CASE STUDY

One story from the trenches before we move on. When I was first starting out as a consultant, I worked with a wonderful midmarket logistics technology company that focused on a specific niche: manufacturers of frozen food that specifically used Microsoft Dynamics as their enterprise resource planning (ERP) program. What a fantastic ICP! We did the TAM analysis, and there were only about 2,500 companies that fit.

Instead of investing heavily in expensive Microsoft value-added reseller shows, I advised them to take a more direct approach: personally reaching out to each of these 2,500 companies. My suggestion was to just call each one!

By targeting a superspecific niche, you can create and deliver content that truly resonates with them and shows how you help solve their problems. Remember, your product or service should be addressing a pain point your ICP needs solving.

LEADING INDICATORS FOR BUYING SIGNALS

Now to further enhance your ability to identify people who are ready to buy, you need to consider tracking and analyzing leading indicators. This allows you to initiate timely and targeted sales conversations, increasing the efficiency of your sales process and the likelihood of converting prospects into customers.

Some effective strategies for identifying leading indicators include:

- Working with sales to analyze past deal data to identify common actions or behaviors that preceded a purchase, including patterns of specific content downloads, webinar attendance, or certain types of inquiries.

- Tracking open and click-through rates of your emails and campaign response rates, particularly for product-focused content.

- Implementing lead scoring, an "out of the box" capability from HubSpot, to assign values to different behaviors and engagement levels. High scores help identify those who are more likely in a decision-making phase.

A NOTE ON *LEAD SCORING*

Lead scoring is a systematic approach for evaluating and ranking prospects against a scale that represents the perceived value each record brings to the organization. It's like having a secret weapon that helps sales and marketing teams prioritize record engagement, respond to buying signals appropriately, and increase the efficacy of sales and marketing efforts.

Components of Lead Scoring

- **Demographics**

Let's talk about the components of lead scoring. It all starts with your ICP and personas. Does the record fit your ICP and an identified persona? We look at the demographic profile of the company ICP and see if it matches the one we're scoring.

- **Behaviors**

Next we've got engagement tracking. We're talking about email opens and clicks, content downloads, webinar attendance, website visits, and social media interaction. These are all signs that the record is interested.

"Lead source" is another key factor. It is how the record came to be in the CRM in the first place. Whether it's organic search, referral, or a paid campaign, the source can give you a clue about the quality of the record. Some sources may consistently produce higher-quality records.

Lastly, the frequency and depth of a record's interaction with your content can also affect scoring. Regular interaction with key content might increase a record's lead score.

A NOTE ON *LEAD SCORING*

- **Lead Scoring in Action**

So how does lead scoring work? You set thresholds for when records are considered "leads" and should be handed off to sales. It's like passing the baton in a relay race but with way more data.

- **Challenges and Considerations**

The effectiveness of lead scoring depends on the accuracy and completeness of the data in your CRM and marketing automation platform. Garbage in, garbage out.

Lead-scoring models need to be dynamic and adaptable to changes in market conditions and customer behavior. You can't set and forget it; it needs to change with the business.

Successful lead scoring requires tight integration with overall sales and marketing processes and alignment between both teams. This is a great opportunity to ingratiate yourself with the sales team.

And remember, your lead score is a leading indicator, but it's not the only buying signal you should be tracking.

- **A Word of Caution**

And always remember that the people who have made it over your arbitrary threshold don't know they've "tripped the wire." Be careful with how you use the proprietary intent data signals you have. Getting an email that says, "We saw you visited our website Sunday at 4:00 p.m.," is pretty creepy. Be thoughtful about how you use your data—people are still people.

Lead scoring is a powerful tool for prioritizing records, aligning sales and marketing efforts, and ultimately driving more efficient conversions. However, it requires ongoing management and refinement to remain effective.

A DOSSIER PER ICP

We're going to talk about account-based marketing (ABM) in depth later, but it makes sense to share a quick note about tracking interest and creating account dossiers to share with your sales team. Trust me, it's worth it.

Building a dossier per future customer is like creating a highly detailed profile that uses lead scoring as a crystal ball to predict their likelihood of buying. This approach is a sophisticated form of lead scoring and customer insight gathering. Here's how you do it:

- Start your prospect dossier by collecting as much information as possible on each prospective company. This should be a piece of cake if you've been on top of your game and created an ICP and tagged them in your HubSpot.

- Do some basic research on each prospect company to understand their challenges, goals, and needs. This may involve analyzing industry trends, reading their press releases and annual reports, and understanding their competitive landscape. You can use AI to help you out. We'll talk more about that in chapter ten.

- Use your lead-scoring model to show all tracked engagement like website visits, email responses, content downloads, and social media engagement.

- Include sales interactions and notes, meetings, or any direct interactions. These provide valuable context that is not captured in digital interactions alone.

- Keep your dossiers updated with any changes in the prospect's business, such as mergers, expansions, or shifts in strategy. You never know how it might affect their needs.

So to sum it up, building a detailed dossier for each potential prospect will help in developing your "in-market" score and allows for more focused, efficient, and personalized sales and marketing efforts. Yes, it requires a commitment to data collection and analysis, but it's going to make your B2B marketing campaigns so much more effective.

EXAMPLE DOSSIER

ACCOUNT NAME

Profile Fit: Strong
Account Reach: High
Buying Stage: Consideration

Vertical: Retail
Account Owner: Bob Smith

10k/Financial Reporting Insights
Goals: Most recent annual report references supply chain sourcing and market expansion
Risks: Company focused on risk mitigation in sustainable supply chain and sourcing

Intent Signals

Robots	Warehouse Solutions	Compliance
Manhattan & Associates	Parts Distribution	Sustainability

Top Pain Points
• Rising Transportation Costs
• Labor Shortages
• Port Congestion
• Global Supply Chain Disruptions
• Increasing Demand for Omni-Channel Fulfillment Options

Top 3 Goals
• Increase Inventory Turnover
• Improve On-Time Delivery Performance
• Implement New Supply Chain Planning System

HOW DOES TRACKING INTEREST GO WRONG?

You may find this hard to believe, but there are companies that do all this work—and never follow up. Tracking interest does not work if there is no follow-up. It can also go wrong if you don't have the right tech stack or are tracking the wrong prospects. Like the entire Revenue Engine framework, all of this is meant to work in conjunction with the other parts.

REVENUE ENGINE RECAP

This chapter covered the critical next phase of our Revenue Engine framework—tracking interest—after initial good news sharing. As discussed, the audience trumps the message itself; even the most effective messaging misses the mark without reaching the right people. Successful tracking requires several key components:

- Defining your TAM provides an essential baseline for monitoring reach and penetration. This evolves over time as personas and products change.

- Ensuring marketing communications extend beyond broad, untargeted blasts to instead cultivate real, live human connections. Two-way engagement with clearly defined niches demonstrates respect and relevance.

- Maintaining meticulous list hygiene sustains the engine; outdated, disjointed databases eventually corrode ROI. This unglamorous but vital process needs embedding into workflows.

- Building an integrated MarTech stack tailored to organizational needs and resources, one-size-fits-none. Prioritize scalable platforms with accessible data and insights.

- Identifying and responding to meaningful behavioral signals amid the noise, quality over quantity. Map interests to needs and route accordingly.

- Scoring leads based on demonstrated buying signs nets actionability. Coupled with intelligent CRM dossiers, sales can prioritize most promising opportunities.

While necessary, these tracking components alone fail to fully ignite the Revenue Engine.

Next we explore the crucial follow-up required to convert interest into pipeline and fuel sustainable growth. The framework comes full circle—without coordinated action across strategy, technology, and teams, even the best-tuned engine sputters.

CHAPTER 3
FOLLOW-UP

WHAT GETS MEASURED GETS MANAGED.

—PETER DRUCKER, *THE PRACTICE OF MANAGEMENT*

Did you hear the one about the company we gave all the leads to and no one ever called them?

Yes, someone from a LeadCoverage customer came to me and expressed frustration that none of our leads had converted. This person had said our leads "weren't worth anything." We gave them lots of good leads, which we could show because we had math to prove it, but their sales team *never followed up on them*, and we had the activity math to prove that too. Sort of defeats the purpose, right?

At LeadCoverage we don't let opportunities like this slip away. We pivoted from the practice of counting on our client's sales team to follow up and created our own sales development rep (SDR) team to bridge the gap between marketing and sales. SDRs are the unsung heroes of the follow-up process, qualifying records and ensuring only the most promising prospects make it through the pipeline.

In this chapter, we'll explore the critical role of follow-up and what it really means:

- Why asking strangers for money is a no-go.

- What the difference is between cold and warm calls.

- How marketing and sales can collaborate for effective follow-up.

- Why you need to nurture your ICPs.

- How ABM and intent data are transforming B2B marketing.

Get ready to dive into the world of follow-up and learn how to turn leads into loyal customers, boosting your revenue in the process. Later, in Part II, we'll take a deep dive into three key components of the Revenue Engine: the prospect funnel, the nurture funnel, and the customer funnel. These are the engine, transforming the fuel, your records, into prospects, and ultimately into happy customers.

DON'T ASK STRANGERS FOR MONEY

You cannot monetize an audience you haven't built.

Here's the thing: you shouldn't ask strangers for money. It's super awkward. Think of it like walking into a bar and approaching the first person you see, and asking, "Would you like to buy me a drink?" Life doesn't work that way—and neither does business.

YOU CAN'T MONETIZE AN AUDIENCE YOU HAVEN'T BUILT.

Donald Miller has a really great piece in *Building a StoryBrand*, where he writes,

> *Us: Will you marry me?*
> *Customer: No*
> *Us: Will you go out with me again?*
> *Customer: Yes*
> *Us: Will you marry me now?*
> *Customer: No*
> *Us: Will you go out with me again?*
> *Customer: Sure, you're interesting and the information you provide is helpful.*
> *Us: Will you marry me?*
> *Customer: OK, I'll marry you now.*[23]

It usually takes more than a first ask to get someone to buy you a drink much less buy whatever product or service you sell. That's where more conversation (follow-up) is so critical.

THE IMPORTANCE OF FOLLOW-UP

Follow-up will dramatically influence the success of a GTM strategy. It transcends mere post-marketing activities, embedding itself as a fundamental element throughout the customer journey. A meticulously crafted follow-up process can be the defining factor that transforms a potential lead into a valuable, long-term customer.

If the GTM strategy is the blueprint for reaching customers and achieving a competitive edge, then follow-up is pivotal for nurturing leads, closing deals, and sustaining customer relationships. Effective follow-up ensures that every opportunity for engagement and conversion is capitalized upon.

Your MarTech system (CRM plus marketing automation) is the backbone of managing follow-up activities, offering a centralized platform to track interactions with prospects and customers. These systems deliver critical insights into customer behavior and preferences, enabling sales and marketing teams to develop more targeted and impactful follow-up strategies.

FOLLOW-UP STRATEGIES

COLD CALLS VERSUS WARM CALLS

We at LeadCoverage do *not* make cold calls, and we don't recommend making cold calls. The ROI is just not there. Cold calls convert at a 2 percent ratio.[24]

Instead, those "buying signals" we discussed in the last chapter come into play here—because what *does* work are warm calls from actual humans. People still buy from people.

There's a little math at play here that we've come to understand in our business. Cold dials will convert from a record to close at 1 to 2 percent. A record who has opened up two or more emails will convert at a 6 percent ratio (getting warmer). It gets better. An individual who shows *real* intent signals, such as regular website visits, form fills, webinar attendance or trade show and making person-to-person contact, will convert to a paying customer 40 percent of the time (much warmer).

That's a pretty big range—2 percent, 6 percent, 40 percent. I think we can all agree that a 2 or 6 percent conversion ratio hardly feels worth it. So instead we focus on the 40 percent conversion. However, to do that you have to have humans who are willing to pick up the phone and build relationships. This isn't a book on sales, but it's essential to master the basics. Following up is the most basic of the basics. In fact it's simply polite communication.

Tracking leading indicators is crucial for gauging the efficacy of follow-up strategies. Leading indicators, including metrics like engagement levels and response times, can predict future sales outcomes. Key performance indicators, such as conversion rates and average deal size, quantify the immediate effects of follow-up efforts. Consistent tracking of these metrics enables businesses to refine their follow-up approaches and align them more closely with overarching business goals.

We will go through these in detail in Part III of the Revenue Engine framework, the three Vs: volume, velocity, and value.

WARMING UP YOUR PROSPECTS

How do you take a record (remember, it's not a lead yet) and warm it up? These are some of the things we've already discussed and all part of the overall approach of this book. You have to share good news about your company—as it pertains to *their* problem needing a solution.

You aren't sharing news that doesn't directly address what your leads care about most. The *quality* of the content matters.

All the work you have done creating your content motion— sharing good news—is put to good use inside your CRM. The content you're sharing is valuable, free, with a point of view, and full of insights. You've established your leadership team as thought leaders, and they're sharing their personal expertise on LinkedIn regularly. It's important that your executive thought leadership (ETL) comes from them, not the company. You've done such a good job positioning your ETL that the press now asks your leaders their opinions on important market-specific topics.

You are setting all this up so that when your SDR makes that inevitable first phone call, the prospect isn't surprised and is happy to learn more. By this point they have interacted with your website, they know who you are, they are following your leaders, or they saw you at a trade show.

This is *monetizing the audience* you have built.

MARKETING + SALES (WORKING TOGETHER) = FOLLOW-UP

As a marketer it is your *job* to care about sales. All the ideas and philosophy and practical advice in this book are only successful if everyone is working toward a common goal. That includes understanding how much revenue needs to be generated to reach those goals and what impact your marketing efforts will have on achieving those goals. We'll talk about this more later in the book, but for now you must *care*. It is easy to be so focused on your marketing efforts that you forget to lift your head up and look at the big picture.

I wish I could say that a disconnect between sales and marketing was rare. But it is not. The two have gone head-to-head for years, with one that was once seen as the revenue generator (sales) and the other as the cost center (marketing). More than once I have had to try to bring these two sides at loggerheads to the table to work together. Instead the "discussion" ends up deadlocked with marketing finding quality leads and sales thinking the leads suck. I've had sales teams literally refuse to call leads. This is a constant refrain in my life when dealing with sales and marketing groups. I'd bet this sounds familiar to you too.

Harvard Business School has a research piece on this called "War between Sales and Marketing." They call out the "cultural conflict between sales and marketing [that] is, if anything, even more entrenched in economic conflict. The two groups' performance is judged very differently. Salespeople make a living by closing sales, full stop. It's easy to see who (and what) is successful almost immediately. But marketing budget is devoted to programs, not people, and it takes much longer to know whether a program has helped to create long-term competitive advantage for the organization."[25] I don't love the image of a war between the groups, but it sure can feel like a battle some days.

But when the groups work together, magic can happen. Real go-to-market success.

One way to look at it is: "Marketing builds brand preference, creates a marketing plan, and generates leads for sales before handing off execution and follow-up tasks to sales."[26] But the other side of that is "marketing's involvement in the sales funnel should be matched by sales' involvement in the upstream, strategic decisions the marketing group is making."[27] The two need to be aligned, working in a symbiotic relationship.

Beware, though, as Conant says, "Sometimes it feels like everyone in the organization is 'on the marketing team.' Because we're all exposed to marketing in our everyday lives, we are biased to believe that we understand marketing—whether or not we have any marketing background or expertise. Which means that CMOs are often fielding opinions and suggestions from people who don't actually know anything about understanding and harnessing the market."[28] Ultimately when this happens, what's important is that you have an informed point of view on the ROI.

NURTURE THAT ICP AS YOU FOLLOW UP

We'll dive a lot deeper into funnels in Part II of our framework, but let's touch on it here as it relates to follow-up.

Nurturing a record, prospect, or even an ICP is a full-team effort. I highly recommend you set some clear KPIs for the time it takes the marketing and sales team to reach out to these groups. This is why a shared database like HubSpot for sales and marketing is my preferred tool. Salesforce software forces the marketing team to live outside the CRM, breaking what should be a seamless integration between the two teams into two separate tasks tracked in separate software. It does nothing but fuel the siloed effect between the two teams.

With HubSpot, you have a single source of truth. After all, you cannot close deals with prospects if you don't have conversations, and you can't monetize an audience that you haven't built. Remember, you should not be trying to squeeze money from strangers.

A FOLLOW-UP STORY FROM THE TRENCHES

In the thick of the pandemic, we worked with our client, GreyOrange, one of the leaders in warehouse robot automation and orchestration to create a series of webinars called Facing the Board. It was 2021 and supply chain professionals were being asked to do insane feats of crazy business acumen and bravery. We all were facing unprecedented challenges. How do you run a manufacturing plant with everyone going home because they're sick? How do you pack orders from a warehouse when everyone has COVID-19? And what about the supply chain? Is it stressed? Can it withstand what the world was experiencing?

These supply chain leaders were being forced to put plans together to address these issues, and then face the board with these plans. Unfortunately none of them had ever been asked to do this before and certainly not from the basement of building B where they rarely saw the light of day. These companies were digging up these supply chain folks, dusting them off, and bringing them to the board meeting to present their plans—in the midst of a global pandemic where so many pieces of it were utterly unpredictable.

That's where we came in.

We held a series of webinars called "Facing the Board," which were meant to help supply chain managers and directors ready themselves to face the scrutiny of the boardroom under the intensity of a global crisis.

We crushed our expectations. First of all it was perfect timing during the pandemic. All these supply chain leaders were facing massive obstacles and hardships. Second we had a point of view on a solution. Finally we knew the target customer intimately. We pitched very specific webinars for a very specific niche facing a very specific kind of board meeting in the very specific pandemic.

We pitched to the right people at the right time.

We sent 280 invites to hyper-specific targets identified on our ICP accounts list. Eighty-four people attended and signed up for one or more webinars. That was a very clear buying signal.

Then we followed up with a call to every single participant.

The results:
- Eighteen meetings with Fortune 100 companies with household names like Nike and Target
- Ten closed deals and an annual run rate of $3 to $10 million per deal
- A total campaign ROI close to $100 million in pipeline value

The takeaway:
The right message at the right time with the right follow-up and the right closers in place leads to success.

INTENT DATA + ABM = THE FUTURE OF B2B MARKETING

Simply put intent data is information collected about someone's online activities and behavior that indicates their level of interest in your product or service. It's essentially digital breadcrumbs that people leave behind as they go about their online activities. Intent data is a significant aspect of modern digital-marketing strategies, particularly in B2B marketing, since analyzing these digital bread-crumbs can lead to a clearer understanding of where your prospects are in their buying journey.

Gartner defines intent data as "a type of sales intelligence that collects online user behavioral data based on interests and analyzes that data to identify accounts that are actively researching on the web."[29]

There are three types of intent data:

First-Party Intent Data: This is data collected from your own website or through direct interactions with potential customers. It can include actions like website page views, downloads, form completions, webinar attendance, email engagement, etc. First-party data is generally more accurate and reliable, as it comes directly from interactions with your own content or platforms. This data lives in your CRM.

You must have an email address in your CRM to be able to track against it. This is why it's so important to own every record you can in your TAM.

Second-Party Intent Data: This type of data is external data typically obtained through a partnership or collaboration with third-party organizations and technology. Second-party data offers a more in-depth view into an account's interests and needs, as it includes engagement metrics from trusted partners who offer complementary solutions. Data collected from programmatic advertising tools and review sites like G2.com, formerly G2 Crowd, and Gartner are used to target programmatic media.

We'll walk through programmatic media versus Google and LinkedIn paid media in detail later in the book, but it's worth a mention here.

In the context of programmatic media buying—a method of purchasing digital advertising space automatically and in real time—secondary intent data becomes a powerful tool. Programmatic media allows us to target only individuals who have demonstrated a relevant interest, even on partner or affiliate sites.

An example: if a prospect engages with content on a *partner's site* like a Capterra, G2 or Gartner, that aligns with your product or service, this engagement, captured as secondary intent data, can be used to target that prospect with specific ads through programmatic buying.

A programmatic approach not only enhances the relevance and effectiveness of the campaigns but also improves the user experience by presenting ads that are more in line with the prospect's demonstrated interests and needs. Consequently, secondary intent data becomes a bridge, connecting your company with a broader yet more targeted audience, making programmatic media buying more efficient and outcome focused.

Third-Party Intent Data: This data is collected from other websites or platforms that are not owned by you but are where potential customers take actions such as downloading content, providing product reviews, and interacting on social media. Often bought from external providers, it helps to broaden your understanding of a prospect's behavior beyond the interactions on your own platform. An easy example of third-party intent data is Bombora, which is based on Google cookies, but new third-party intent tools pop up every day, and you can often access intent inside your data tool, like SalesIntel.

By leveraging all three types of intent data, you will have a more holistic understanding of each potential customer's intent, enabling more personalized and timely engagement. It can guide decisions about which leads sales should prioritize, what content marketing should be developed, where and how to engage with prospects at the right time with the right message, and how to tailor offerings to match potential customers' needs and interests.[30]

There are only a very small handful of players in this market. They call themselves ABM software. These tools are incredible. They give you so much insight into what your potential customers are doing, as well as what your current customers are doing, what they're searching for, whether or not they're in a buying cycle with someone else, and more.

These are super valuable, next-level tools. I think intent data is the future of B2B marketing, and when combined with the AI tools that we're seeing come out now, they are going to change the way we market.

The democratization of intent data tools is coming at us fast. At the time of writing, top-tier intent data tools like DemandBase and 6sense are only accessible to the enterprise-level companies due to their costs, which can run from $80,000 to upward of $100,000 per year. And you also need a full-time human to run these tools.

We've found a second tier of intent tools that include programmatic media buying starting to pop up. Plus, there are a growing number of "dip your toe in the water" tools we're seeing success with for a moderate month-to-month investment.

It all reminds me that when I started my career, Salesforce didn't exist. (Yes, I know I'm aging myself here.) Those of us who were creative and thinking along the lines of measurement were making our own CRMs out of access databases just because we needed *something*.

HubSpot, way back when, started as a marketing automation tool with a free CRM. Over time the democratization of those tools and the disruptors of those tools became much more accessible for the small and medium businesses (SMB) and midmarket.

We're just on the cusp of that with intent data. As economist and professor Theodore Levitt says, "Never before have companies had such powerful technologies for interacting directly with customers, collecting and mining information about them, and tailoring their offers accordingly." And that is and will be one of the things we're going to see disrupt and transform B2B GTM.

REVENUE ENGINE RECAP

This chapter focused on the critical role of follow-up in the Revenue Engine framework. After sharing good news and tracking interest, follow-up is essential for nurturing leads, closing deals, and maintaining customer relationships. Pure and simple. But if that follow-up is sloppy, inconsistent, or nonexistent, it'll render all your efforts useless.

A few key takeaways from this chapter:

- You can't ask strangers for money. Building relationships and trust with potential customers is crucial.

- Cold calls are not and never will be a good use of your time. Leads who have shown interest through various interactions (e.g., website visits, form fills, webinar attendance) are more likely to convert.

- Marketing and sales teams must work together. Hard stop. If you want to ensure effective follow-up, a seamless integration between the two teams is essential for success.

- Nurturing your ICP is a full-team effort that requires setting clear KPIs for follow-up time.

Mark my words: the future of B2B GTM is all about intent data and ABM. And it's coming fast.

We've made it through to the end of Part I. You now have had a primer on my framework. And we're just getting started!

Now it's time to build and care for funnels in Part II.

PART II

THE FUNNELS

LIFE ITSELF IS A FUNNEL OF DECISIONS, AND SO IS BUSINESS. AT EACH STAGE, WHAT WE CHOOSE TO FOCUS ON AND IMPROVE DICTATES OUR DIRECTION.

—SIMON SINEK

Like Simon Sinek says, essentially life is a funnel. In our Revenue Engine framework specifically, we have narrowed our work down to three funnels:

- The prospect funnel which measures your awareness activities.

- The nurture funnel which measures your marketing activity ROI.

- The customer funnel which measures your current customer cross-sell and upsell opportunities.

To illustrate how everything is a funnel, let me first tell you about how I trapped my husband into marrying me.

When I met my husband, he was a stranger. At the time, he really was nothing more than a prospect who I "qualified" like any lead—and he was everything I wanted in a future spouse. He was a catch who fit my ICP. A nuclear engineer slash fitness model (no, I'm not kidding), he was 100 percent my top prospect. Eventually he moved from a prospect to the nurture funnel, and we were officially a couple.

We had been dating for about two years when I started training for the 2009 Ironman Wisconsin. Ironman training is very, very selfish. You spend a lot of time by yourself swimming, cycling, or running—all with your headphones in. Meanwhile, we had been discussing marriage, and he said we would get engaged after the Ironman. In my twenty-six-year-old brain, I heard "at the finish line of the Ironman." Obviously.

I did *not* get a diamond ring at the finish line. There was no waiting string quartet with my then-boyfriend on bended knee and all our friends and family there to celebrate. I might add, "Thank goodness." Because you look and smell like a wreck at the end of a 2.4-mile swim, a 112-mile bike ride, and a 26.2-mile run. So that scenario could have gone horribly wrong had he not had the good sense to wait. But my twenty-six-year-old brain desperately wanted a ring.

Four weeks later Echo Global Logistics, where I worked, went public. My name was on the IPO press release. It was a big damn deal. Here I am, an Ironman, and now I am a part of my company's IPO. I was in the best shape of my life. I was a beloved spin teacher. I owned my own house—in my twenties! My career was skyrocketing. At that moment my value on the Chicago dating market was ten out of ten.

I was driven then as much as I am driven now. Today I'm a successful entrepreneur. I concepted, developed, formulated, and implemented this framework many times over. I wrote this book! I didn't just acquire this personality yesterday. At the time of my Ironman and the IPO, I had a life plan: married before I turned thirty, first baby by thirty-two.

Do not mess with this type-A chick's goals.

While in the relationship nurture funnel, my then-boyfriend (not yet even a fiancé) bought himself a nice watch—*before* an engagement ring.

Excuse me? When I gave him a hard time about my conspicuously bare ring finger on my left hand, he acted nonchalantly. "Calm down. I promise, we'll get engaged," he had said. So I did what every normal girl would do.

I booked the church.

The priest at my parents' church congratulated me on my engagement. I informed him that, actually, I wasn't engaged. I told him that if the proposal never happened, he could keep the hundred bucks it took to reserve the church.

Next I took all the magnets, photos, and papers off my fridge. Cleared it completely—except for the receipt from the church.

One night my now-husband (and yes, despite my nuttiness on this issue, he *did* propose) leaned in, and he asked, "Hey, what is this thing on your fridge?" He was referring, of course, to the giant 8.5 x 11 receipt in the center of the door.

"I forgot to tell you! I booked the church for my wedding."

"What wedding?"

"My wedding," I said. "In 264 days. Right now I am a ten, and if you're not going to marry me, I will find someone else." Because after all, I was a triathlete, spin instructor, homeowner, and successful career woman, and waiting was not an option. (I'm also funny and charming when I want to be.)

Two weeks later we were engaged. We're still happily married. That deal is still the best hard close of my life.

Obviously I was not planning to marry a stranger, which is where prospects begin. As he moved to the nurture funnel, he'd sent me *many* buying signals over three years. He just needed a little push to make it into my customer funnel.

This whole playful story uses dating in Chicago in your twenties as an analogy because it feels very much like a sales funnel. You meet a bunch of strangers, you send them through the funnel, and you disqualify most. You say no thank you to more, you lose some deals you had hoped to close (the one that got away, anyone?), and depending on the value of the goods you're selling, you can decide on what your ICP is, and then you nurture them until the customer comes through. Then you seal the deal.

In the next chapter we'll look at the funnel concepts as they apply to marketing, sales—and measuring success. (Plus, we'll do some math!)

CHAPTER 4

THE PROSPECT FUNNEL

IDENTIFYING IN-MARKET ACCOUNTS IS KEY TO MAKING
MEANINGFUL CHANGES IN YOUR SALES AND MARKETING.

—LATANÉ CONANT

A funnel, at its simplest, is the process of elimination. The prospect funnel is a strategic approach to identifying and engaging with the records that show the most promise of becoming a customer. Like I did in my refrigerator receipt story, you are essentially in the process of disqualifying cold leads when you're in the prospect funnel.

In this chapter, we'll explore:

- The power of splitting the traditional funnel into three distinct segments.

- The significance of flexion points between funnels.

- Top-of-funnel campaign strategies and reengaging cold leads.

- Advanced prospecting funnels, ABM, and intent data.

- The importance of disqualification in optimizing conversion rates.

We'll dive into strategies for grabbing the attention of ideal customers, reengaging cold leads, and leveraging advanced tactics like ABM and intent data. Fun fact: there is power in disqualification when you realize the *who* is more important than the *what*.

As we guide records through the prospect funnel, steering them toward becoming qualified leads, we'll set the stage for the next phase and next chapter, the nurture funnel, where relationship building takes center stage.

WHY THE REVENUE ENGINE SPLITS THE FUNNEL INTO THIRDS

Most sales and marketing books will simplify the sales funnel into one continuous funnel that moves prospects from awareness to conversion to loyalty. I believe that doesn't leave room for the nuances of the customer journey, and it leaves out the subtleties and uniqueness of how GTM teams should be engaging with prospects. There is also a big difference in the content we use in a conversation with a stranger versus a prospect close to closing or a current customer.

So in our framework, we split the funnel into thirds to more easily define the movement from stranger to customer.

THE PROSPECT FUNNEL

In the prospect funnel, records start as strangers. Your total addressable market (TAM) is where your funnel starts. After all, your Revenue Engine needs fuel and records from your TAM is the gas you pump into the tank. The number of records in your prospect funnel should change all the time. The count of records at the top of the prospect funnel should be your most fluid KPI.

This is where you're going to put the TAM analysis from Part I to work.

In the TAM, you identify *all* the people who could potentially become customers, then you send them the good news that we talked about in chapter one. When you own the records of the humans at the accounts that are ICPs in your CRM tool, you can track their activity around your good news properly.

The simplest example: You send a list of records your good news. In this case let's use the new Gartner analyst report that profiles your business and its new offering. After seeing your news, your target prospect shows up to a landing page or to your webinar, they open an email, or you see them at a trade show, etc. The record's activity, the breadcrumbs, are recorded inside your CRM. Those little breadcrumbs are the clues you need to follow to move those records through our funnels and then into actual customers.

The road to revenue is paved with buying signals.

In the prospect funnel, we have some assumed characteristics we've attributed to these records from third-party sources like SalesIntel or ZoomInfo, but we have no clear indication they have a problem we can solve or if they're interested in our solution. However, as these records move through our prospect funnel, we *will* acquire primary intent signals and learn more and more about both the ICP and the persona for the record.

For records to make it to the bottom of the prospect funnel, we identify that they meet the key criteria to go from "record" to "prospect." Every GTM team's criteria is different, so you should decide on these as a team. Key criteria guidelines include:

1. Confirmation the company fits our ICP.

2. The record has shown enough intent for us to be confident in assuming they know who we are.

3. Their lead score reaches the "nurture" threshold (more on building a lead score threshold).

NOW THEY'RE LEADS

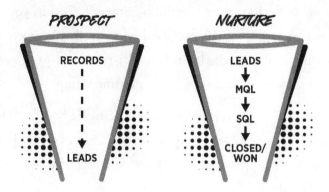

As your records start to show signs of interest, and you've decided they are now aware of your company, we've reached an important point in our prospect's journey: the flexion point.

THE MAGIC OF THE FLEXION POINT

This flexion point is where the magic happens in the Revenue Engine. In the traditional funnel, there are no "breaks" to measure. No opportunities to check your work and change strategies if needed. We built the Revenue Engine model to identify and focus on these flexion points—to take a break and assess, disqualify, and be intentional about which records deserve to be in your funnel.

This flexion point is important for three reasons:

1. The movement from one funnel to the next is an excellent way to "check your work." Are your ICP definitions clear?

Are the records that matriculate through the prospect funnel the right prospects? Who can you disqualify?

2. These flexion points should be time stamped in your CRM so you can pull reports based on *when* they happen. (More on measuring velocity in Part III.) The velocity of movement in your funnels is dependent on time stamps.

3. Accountability is easier when you have clearly defined funnels and funnel stages. Without these flexion points, it can be confusing to the marketing and sales teams who owns what and when.

As you track your prospects, the "magic" is in the measurement of the deltas. A delta is the rate of change from one state to another. When a stranger starts at the top of our funnel, we are looking for the rate of change to the bottom of the funnel. When the record moves from the prospect to the nurture funnel, we have our first flexion point. How many make it, and how fast? Having a flexion point to measure gives you an easy KPI to share with leadership and benchmark against.

We will have a marketing math lesson, which I promise will not be painful, at the beginning of Part III. For now you just have to remember that a delta represents the rate of change.

Breaking up the traditional funnel may feel foreign to some executives. That's OK, share your point of view and what you expect to be able to measure more effectively by adding delta measurements between funnels. The goal is to get your sales and marketing leadership aligned on what good looks like.

What good looks like will be different in every company. One company may say the bar for tipping the flexion point from prospect to the nurture funnel is as low as opening an email. Another company may require a record jump through more hoops and request an actual quote or fill out a form. No matter what the buying signals you want these records to show you, don't forget: you aren't asking for money yet.

Records that have reached the bottom of the prospect funnel can now be called "leads." But not all leads are equal.

THE THREE FUNNELS

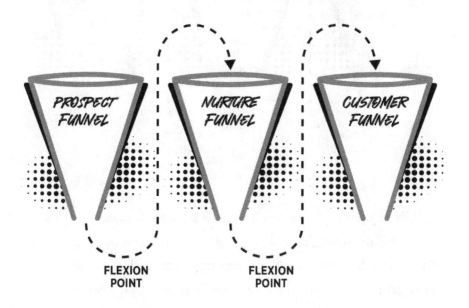

A record enters the prospect funnel and ends as a lead, assuming it makes its way all the way down through the funnel and past the flexion point. When the lead is then put into the top of the nurture funnel, it becomes a marketing qualified lead (MQL). The MQL becomes a sales qualified lead (SQL) when it gets to the bottom of the nurture funnel and the flexion point tips once again. The SQL is ready for closing and to become a customer. A customer ready for cross-sell and upsell opportunities.

THE REVENUE ENGINE

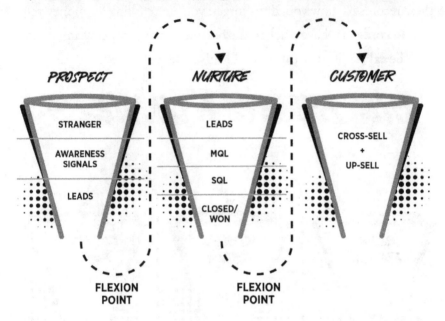

By separating these motions into separate functions, you can apply specific strategies and campaigns to a hyper-focused group of records. Each campaign needs a hypothesis and goal. A top-of-funnel prospecting campaign goal is to drive those records deeper into your prospecting funnel.

TOP-OF-FUNNEL (TOF) CAMPAIGN STRATEGIES AND IDEAS

Top-of-funnel (TOF) means exactly what it says—the beginning, or top, of the prospect funnel. The most important thing to keep in mind when creating TOF campaigns for the prospect funnel is that every customer begins the journey as a stranger. In the opening pages of Conant's book, she reminds readers: Don't forget a prospect is a future customer—engage accounts, not leads.[31] I connect deeply to the idea that prospects are *future customers*. The top of the prospecting funnel should be the largest stage you have by record count. Remember, we're executing a process of elimination. The top of the prospecting funnel is where you are looking for and tracking the smallest signal that your future customers know who you are.

Conant makes another very important point. You are tracking companies through the prospect funnel, not humans. This may feel counterintuitive because we market to humans, but we are selling to businesses in B2B. When you deliver the KPIs and math-driven leading indicators to your board (more on that later), the board doesn't ask how many people you are reaching, they want to know the number of companies that are showing interest.

While we, as marketers, need to be aware and build campaigns and content for humans, we need to keep in mind the ever-present guiding light: revenue is the goal and revenue comes from companies. Humans in those companies will sign on the dotted line, but the opportunity will be viewed at the company level by your leadership team, so build your funnels to provide reporting that will matter in the boardroom.

As I have said before, you can't ask strangers for money. I mean, you can, but that is rude. You don't walk into a coffee shop and ask the guy behind you to buy your coffee. You don't walk into a room of people you don't know and ask everyone for a thousand dollars. And you don't call a business stranger and ask them to sign a contract without developing a relationship.

You can't monetize relationships you haven't built.

Mass email blasting a bunch of strangers asking for their time, energy, or money is a recipe for failure (and an example of RAOM). Thus the first section of the book included "share good news" as one of our framework's tenets. We're trying to move someone from "I've never heard of you" to "I *know* who you are" by offering news, information, and thought leadership that these potential customers really and truly need and want. Going from unknown to known, then from known to expert. At the TOF, you are dealing with total strangers, and you can't market to strangers the same way you would market to people who know who you are or to those who have shown a buying signal.

DEVELOPING AWARENESS AND INTEREST

Our "share good news" philosophy creates multiple opportunities to drive awareness at the TOF for strangers. This is crucial for laying the groundwork for building relationships that can be monetized. Good news inherently attracts attention, as we've discussed. In a business environment often saturated with aggressive sales pitches and technical jargon, a breath of positive news can be refreshing and engaging. It shows you value the person reading your good news more than the transaction that will be the result. Such content not only intrigues potential customers, but also helps in establishing credibility and a positive brand perception. Plus, people are more likely to organically share good news content than they would share a sales pitch.

We can also use good news to drive multichannel content delivery, which is just consulting jargon for "saying the same thing a whole bunch of ways." Utilizing a multichannel approach ensures that the message reaches a wider audience. Your online messaging may reach as little as 1 to 2 percent of your audience. You need to repeat your messaging on a variety of channels, and you need to do it more than you might think.

EXAMPLES OF TOP-OF-FUNNEL PROSPECT CAMPAIGNS TO DRIVE AWARENESS:

1. Case Studies and Success Stories

2. Analysts Reports and Surveys

3. Email Newsletters and LinkedIn Newsletters

4. Webinars and Workshops

5. Long-Form Content Marketing (Blogs, E-books, Whitepapers)

6. Social Media Campaigns

7. Search Engine Optimization (SEO) and Paid Search Advertising (PPC) (more on this later)

8. Influencer Collaborations and Podcasts

9. Partnership Announcements and Collaborations

10. Free Tools and Trials

Building awareness is building an audience who is interested in the next thing you have to say.

CAMPAIGN STRUCTURE

No matter the campaign you choose or the content that is delivered, every campaign must have a hypothesis, goals, and a way to track the interest of your audience then a clear follow-up strategy.

REENGAGING AND RESURRECTING "COLD RECORDS"

Inevitably there are records that stop engaging with your content. If they clearly fit your ICP, you can execute what we at LeadCoverage call an "awakening" or "signs of life" campaign. "Dead" or "cold" records are records that haven't engaged with any of our content in six or more months. If you're unsure if a record is "dead," simply look at the record's last activity date from the time stamps in your CRM.

If you want to engage and resurrect these leads, follow this multistep process:

Step 1: Clean that list! Don't let a campaign created for cold records damage your domain authority by sending it to a bunch of email addresses that shouldn't be in your CRM anyway. But "cold records" should still fit your ICP. In fact, the prospect funnel will be the dirtiest funnel you have, and it should be the dirtiest. When I say "dirty," I mean records who may be the wrong ICP, are too old, or just aren't ever going to become a customer. The prospect funnel is a good place to experiment with new markets or dream ICPs. Plus, it's a good place to put all those trade show records the sales team comes back with. You just need to clean it up, so to speak.

Step 2: Create a three-email campaign with a simple message, less than thirty words, and ideally from a human, not necessarily an executive, to a small group of records you'd like to engage.

Step 3: Watch closely for signs of life, including emails that are opened or are clicked through or receive a reply.

Spoiler alert: We see an average of 2 to 10 percent "awakening" when executing this against "cold" or "dead" lists. Hence the "awakening" or "signs of life" campaign names. But don't set yourself up to fail by telling your leadership team there are a bunch of leads in this list—there aren't. Not yet.

USING ADVANCED PROSPECTING FUNNELS PLUS ABM AND INTENT DATA

You know what's sexy? Having access to intent signals from our TOF prospects without having to actually touch the records. Intent data and ABM software give us access to those signals and we can watch records drive themselves down the funnel.

What is even sexier is connecting the movement of records you haven't touched but that have reacted to your sharing good news. It's a strategy that is coming for us all and is one that works. Yes, I'm aware that thinking this is sexy makes me a supernerd. I'm owning it.

A DISCUSSION ON TRACKING HUMAN ACTIVITY OR COMPANY ACTIVITY

In my consulting practice, one of the first decisions we make with clients is what will be tracked in their funnel. In other words, "What is the math your leadership wants to see?"

In B2B marketing we can track the math, or activity, in two ways: by human activity and by company activity. Companies may buy from companies, but humans make those buying decisions. It's important to track and report on both.

But if we had to choose between the two, nine out of ten times we'd recommend primarily tracking company activity. Companies will move through the nurture funnel to become customers, so you'll track company activity in your reports.

Let's say you are tracking Bob Smith from Nike, and all the tracking breadcrumbs are tied to Bob for your deal. But Bob suddenly takes new job at Adidas. Is your deal with Nike dead? No. *But your activity reporting is.* And now you have a new opportunity with Bob at Adidas, which can create a real reporting headache.

This is why we recommend working backward from the reports your leadership team wants to see. Sit down with your sales leadership partner and have a conversation about which leading indicators will indicate interest inside the companies you want to track.

In this way you are treating your prospecting funnel almost like a B2C engagement. Your lists can involve lots of people from different types of companies all getting a similar message because you are just looking for signals that they know who you are. Later in the nurture funnel chapter is where we'll continue the conversation on building company dossiers.

PAID MEDIA AS A GTM STRATEGY

Paid media is an important part of any GTM strategy, but it has a specific set of rules and should be thought of as a tactic in a larger strategy. I've asked Courtney Herda, our head of paid media at LeadCoverage, to walk us through paid media, specifically Google, LinkedIn, and programmatic advertising.

POWERFUL PAID MEDIA STRATEGY

CONTRIBUTION BY COURTNEY HERDA, HEAD OF PAID MEDIA AT LEADCOVERAGE

Paid advertising provides the opportunity to promote your brand, increase traffic to your website or landing page, and engage with your ICPs in a range of different forms including video, text, and images. Your advertisements will then be displayed on search engines, social media platforms, websites, and beyond. It works quickly, costs are easy to control, and metrics are relatively easy to measure and interpret.

However, a common misconception is that paid ads are exclusively a "spray and pray" effort. I can tell you right now that no amount of keyword research will magically uncover the keyword that the CEO or head of the buying committee at your target enterprise prospect is googling. If you expect this, and worse, if you promise this to the C-suite, you will be disappointed by the results. Decision makers at the enterprise level are rarely doing their own research, certainly not at the preliminary or awareness stages. This is why a detailed understanding of the funnel, how it works, and your ICP is key to success.

Modern consumer behavior is not a straight line. Our B2B sales cycle might be a funnel to us, but the actual buying experience includes anywhere from a dozen to nearly a hundred touchpoints, including countless journeys across multiple channels and platforms, and in-person, trade show, website, and video engagements. No B2B buyer doing research on your company thinks to themselves, "Oh, great, now I'm going to be an SQL in this company's nurture funnel! I can't wait for the follow-up." Buyers research for all sorts of reasons, and we use paid media to improve the chances of your message reaching the right persona at the right stage with the right message. We do of course use paid media to facilitate awareness, influence consideration, and ultimately drive revenue.

BUILDING AWARENESS: DISPLAY ADVERTISING

As we've discussed, cold leads are not buyers, and unless you're selling socks, your persona is not going to slide through the funnel and transact on your website. So we like to start with awareness campaigns. Like driving past a billboard each morning, branded display ads on relevant sites create awareness and familiarity. At this point, your target persona may not be in the market. They may not even be aware that they have a problem. But display ads have a very broad reach that places impressions where your customers are browsing; we can target similar searches, lookalike audiences, pull lists from offline or third-party sources, or use keyword targeting. With a range of formats, we're able to serve "online billboards" as users move around the web. Awareness-focused ads often highlight industry challenges and introduce innovative solutions, targeting the broader audience.

Now our buying committee is aware of a problem and a potential solution. They might also be aware of your brand. This facilitates the search process, and buyers, or more often the people who work for buyers, are often driven to "Google it." A key component of tracking interest is reaching a real, live breathing human. So the most important question is: Where are your humans, and what are they searching for?

The *who* is more important than the *what*.

How does your *who* formulate searches? Are they searching on desktops or mobile devices? Are they using voice search? Are they video watchers on YouTube? Blog or news readers? We're back to understanding the ICP and persona. These components help inform everything from messaging to keyword lists to ad format.

CONSIDERATION ADS: CAPTURING INTENT

Marketers love an 80/20 rule, and paid ads are no different. Eighty percent of searches are done on the most general terms. Twenty percent are done on very specific terms. As users move through the funnel and conduct research, keywords get more refined, more specific, and more targeted on pain points or solutions. It's vital to make sure your ads appear in every situation so you can help facilitate their education and capture their intent cues. These consideration ads can provide in-depth content, case studies, analyst reports, or product demos to establish credibility and demonstrate value. Furthermore, once your buying committee has identified your brand as a contender, they're going to be looking up your brand and your competitors' brands, so ensuring you show up when they search is imperative.

DECISION-BASED ADS: DRIVING CONVERSIONS

At this point you've driven traffic to your website or landing page on a range of search queries. You've created solution and brand awareness. This is when the magic happens. Paid ads are never successful in a silo, so we're going to continue to create top-of-mind signals across our paid channels that move records through the funnel. These decision-based ads focus on driving conversions by offering special promotions, consultations, or trial periods. Depending on the makeup of your ICP or your buying committee, ads may appear on YouTube, LinkedIn, Google, or display and programmatic networks. We'll amplify good news with sponsored posts and leverage trade show opportunities with paid media. The makeup of your personas is what dictates the specifics, the messaging, and the frequency.

ALWAYS-ON ADVERTISING

But your job as a marketer isn't done as soon as the customer is marked "closed won." Ads that provide further value can contribute to upsell and cross-sell opportunities. Ads that create "delight" can turn customers into fans and cheerleaders, and these are crucial in cementing success.

MEASUREMENT

But now we return to the math. One of the greatest benefits of paid ads is that they are infinitely measurable. However, in a complicated buying cycle with dozens of touchpoints, clear ROI attribution is harder than you'd think. Paid ad platforms lean on a word that means both everything and nothing at the same time, "conversions." Conversions are not necessarily leads, but all paid ad leads start as conversions. Until you have them tracked and quality checked, they're just confirmation that your ad led to something. Warning: Don't let the C-suite get hung up on the word "conversion" in paid ads. Have a point of view on what it means to you, as the word "conversion" is misleading.

Getting a budget for paid ads is entirely dependent on the math. This is where tying ad campaigns into your CRM allows you to follow the attribution chain and better understand the path to purchase and the role paid ads play in your sales cycle. As that record moves from paid ad conversion to MQL to SQL to a closed won client, the role paid ads plays evolves.

PROGRAMMATIC ADVERTISING: THE FUTURE OF PAID MEDIA

While a portion of your paid media budget should always be spent on owning your own brand (buying your own company name, etc.) using display ads and the always-improving motion of the consideration and decision-based digital spend, building a programmatic display engine is the future of B2B digital marketing.

Programmatic advertising is part of an ABM motion—more on that in a later chapter—and requires a third-party tool to execute. Programmatic ad spend uses what you've learned from Google and LinkedIn plus your very specific ICP and target list to target *just* the buyers you've identified at your target prospect.

The third-party programmatic tools allow us to hyper-target individuals inside a company with ads based on their buying signals so far. It's creepy, yes. But very effective and inexpensive. We have a case study on a buyer clicking a programmatic ad for a hyper-specific product valued at tens of millions for less than $1.

If your current paid advertising team isn't recommending a programmatic approach, it's time to bring it up. One of the big problems we see is B2B companies using traditional B2C paid media teams to run their paid programs. Paid media expertise on selling socks will not translate to selling integrated supply chain management services to enterprise buyers.

Strategic implementation of paid ads, tailored to the different stages of the customer journey and informed by intelligent targeting and your tech stack, can strengthen your position as an industry thought leader, drive engagement, and ultimately contribute to sustained business growth.

THE POWER OF DISQUALIFICATION

We've talked about prospect funnel, flexion points, and some campaign strategies. Each of which requires considering who (still more important than what) you're communicating to and tracking on your journey to qualifying. At this point, I want to let you in on one more thing: Disqualification is just as powerful a tool as qualification.

You're probably thinking, "Wait. What?" I get it. Maybe your team has been devotees of the spray-and-pray method Courtney mentioned where you are constantly trying to reach as many people as possible and oversaturate them with messages on all channels. But the Revenue Engine and LeadCoverage point of view is disqualification can be just as valuable as qualifying prospects.

That deserves another round: Disqualifying prospects can be just as valuable as qualifying prospects. In fact, you should be adding records into the top of this prospecting funnel and getting increasingly clear about these prospects over time so you can *disqualify* them. It saves time and energy throughout the GTM process. I know this can be a tricky thing to present to leadership. But it's math! And you need that math if you want to be considered to be qualified (see what I did there?) for an executive level role.

Here's an example from my supply chain vertical. There are 19,677 shippers in the United States with over $100 million in revenue. The same math exists for your niche: manufacturing, oil and gas, tech, etc. This is true for any B2B industry. Those are some large numbers, and you need to get your hands on them.

The reality is that not all of those 19,677 shippers are the right customer for you. It is your job as the marketer or GTM pro to make sure that you acquire the records, the TAM, either through your company's efforts or the purchase of lists. It is then your job to *disqualify* those in the TAM that you know are *not* appropriate to market to because they are not going to buy from you.

At this point it is highly likely you are now thinking, "Right, lady. My boss is going to tell me I need to continue to market to them." It is your job to have a point of view about why you are *not* going to continue to market to everyone on earth and why you have disqualified a portion of the TAM.

You're right. When you tell an executive that the TAM is a nudge under twenty thousand companies, chances are they are going to ask you why twenty thousand companies are not in the database. There is often an unspoken (or spoken) expectation for you to have every single record in your database. Your answer should be, "We have a clear ideal customer profile and we have disqualified 20 percent [or your number] based on our ICP characteristics. Our remaining TAM is sixteen thousand companies that fit our ICP."

You should be qualifying those records (remember, they are records because they are still strangers) on a regular basis through this funnel. Less sophisticated executives might tell you to market to everyone in the TAM. "Send the emails to everyone!" If you don't really know what you are doing, it sounds sort of reasonable. Why not? What's the harm?

The harm is that this is a major RAOM. Do not do this—*ever*! RAOMs are like dumping a pile of LEGO bricks on someone who only needed a single tan rectangle. Now they're sitting and standing and walking on hundreds of LEGO bricks, hurting their feet and cursing you out the whole time. They didn't need all the LEGO bricks. Just like you don't need to send all the emails to everyone ever.

If you "spray and pray," you're forgetting that the *who* is more important than the *what*. You're wasting more time and energy and resources blasting twenty thousand companies when your time, energy, and resources would be far better spent creating an ICP to get the *who* perfect.

You should be touching and tracking these ICP strangers. You should be looking for buying signals that trigger a flexion point and then matriculate those ready for the nurture funnel.

USING YOUR PROSPECT FUNNEL AS A TOOL

We can use the prospecting funnel to help narrow down an ICP. Often we see ICPs that are too broad because those less-sophisticated leadership teams don't want to "give up" on any opportunities (even the wrong ones) to get hyper-targeted on the right opportunities. To go back to my dating analogy, those teams are spending thousands and thousands of dollars on first dates, making small talk with thousands of people night after night, when they're really looking for a partner they want to settle down with but never find because they're so busy buying the first round with a stranger.

Some simple back-of-the-napkin math can often help to illustrate how a targeted approach is more valuable in the long term: If your goal is $50 million in deals, you can do fifty deals for a million each. Or five deals of $10 million. Or one huge deal. (We will discuss this more in our Volume, Velocity, and Value chapters in Part III.) An ideal customer might purchase on the high end.

Someone who doesn't fit your profile at all will buy exactly zero. (Remember, the BEST, most award-winning supply chain marketing campaign won't move any needles if it's pitched to my mother-in-law.)

CASE STUDY

Our SaaS client sells a very specific software as a service (names redacted to protect the innocent). We had fine-tuned their ICP to the midmarket. The Revenue Engine was working, and we had math to prove it. Then one of their C-suite leaders suggested they pursue a huge enterprise company because of a C-suite relationship. Definitely not the midmarket ICP we had identified.

The unified sales and marketing team did their best to make it clear that there was no sense prospecting this logo because our ICP and product market fit was midmarket. But this C-suite executive was adamant. "Get me in front of them, and we'll close it. It will be a game changer."

It took months to find the right contacts and to build a campaign based on an enterprise target with new content and language. More time getting in front of the right persona and showing them a demo—only to find out that the targeted enterprise company had no use case for this software after all. We had wasted our time and energy chasing a sexy logo that wasn't in our ICP. Yes, one of their C-suite execs went to college with their economic buyer, but it didn't pan out because it simply didn't make sense. And we had known it.

Sound familiar?

There is an opportunity cost to the organization when marketing and sales activities are expended going after accounts that are not a clear ICP fit. Probably the most important principle that a sophisticated sales leader understands is value per deal, which we will talk about in the value chapter in Part III. Good leaders will have the guts to shut down sales engagement opportunities if the ICP is not a perfect fit. I see sales leaders who continue to push the marketing and sales teams to pursue logos that are a bad fit from the beginning entirely too often. To this executive, activity is more important than value.

REVENUE ENGINE RECAP

We've made it to the bottom of our first funnel, the prospect funnel. This is where records start as strangers and are eventually transformed into leads. The chapter emphasized the importance of disqualification and targeting the right prospects, as well as the significance of the flexion point between funnels.

Your key takeaways from this chapter:

- The Revenue Engine framework splits the traditional funnel into three parts (the Prospect, Nurture, and Customer Funnels) to better define the movement from stranger to customer.

- The flexion point between funnels is where the "magic" happens, as it allows for checking the clarity of ideal customer profile (ICP) definitions, measuring velocity, and ensuring accountability.

- Top-of-funnel campaign strategies include awareness and interest campaigns, tracking executive thought leadership

(ETL), AR, PR, and trade shows, reengaging cold records and paid media.

- Advanced prospecting funnels can leverage ABM and intent data to drive prospects through the funnel more efficiently.

- Disqualification is a powerful tool for saving time and resources by focusing on the right prospects that fit the ICP.

Remember: Focusing on the right prospects can save time, energy, and resources throughout the GTM process. Like when you're dating, you need to have a clear understanding of your ideal customer. You don't want to waste your weekends with someone who isn't right for you. You also must have the courage to disqualify prospects who don't align with your ICP, even if they seem like attractive opportunities at first glance.

Now let's turn those leads into prospects ready to make a purchase.

CHAPTER 5

THE NURTURE FUNNEL

IN HIGH-PRODUCTIVITY SALES ORGANIZATIONS, SALESPEOPLE DO NOT CAUSE CUSTOMER ACQUISITION GROWTH, RATHER THEY FULFILL IT.

—AARON ROSS, *PREDICTABLE REVENUE*

The B2B customer journey is notoriously long. It's also complex and ever-changing. Because of this, your prospects need a guiding hand to lead them through it. That's where you come in.

The three Revenue Engine funnels are one-way streets, and your goal is to keep those prospects moving forward through them, no matter what. The nurture funnel in particular is the crucial bridge between the prospect's first spark of interest and the moment they sign on the dotted line.

In this chapter, we'll dive into the nurture funnel and see how it differs from the prospect and customer funnels. We'll answer the question that came up earlier about whether you should track companies or individual contacts.

Plus, I'll help you figure out what's best for you, so you can focus on what—and who—really matters. You'll learn about excellent, real-world examples of nurture campaigns and more best practices.

Future customers go on an intricate journey from awareness to decision-making. It's your job to help them stay on track by setting realistic expectations and providing accurate data and intelligence to help effectively guide those clients through the nurture funnel and into the customer funnel.

In this chapter, you'll get the insights you need to make informed decisions and watch leads transform into prospects who are ready to buy. And once they're customers? That's a whole other funnel we'll do a deep dive into in the next chapter.

But first let's spend a few minutes on the *real* difference between those three funnels.

THE PROSPECT FUNNEL

The goal of the prospect funnel is to separate the records (strangers) at the top of your GTM effort and put them neatly in marketing's court to manage when they leave as leads. These strangers react to the good news you share with the marketplace. Little by little they're learning more about you through that good news and your executives share their point of view on every channel possible.

THE NURTURE FUNNEL

The nurture funnel is where things start to get interesting. Once a record has made it through the prospect funnel and becomes a lead, you'll have a list of characteristics about this ICP-confirmed target account. You can use these characteristics as the foundation for developing and sharing related pain-specific content through all your channels. The goal of the nurture funnel is to take ICPs who know who you are and turn them into opportunities for your sales team to close. The MQLs become SQLs which then become opportunities.

THE CUSTOMER FUNNEL

The customer funnel is self-explanatory. Once you have closed an opportunity with an account, the next step is to cross-sell and upsell them into using more of your services. This is usually a huge gap for marketing teams. We're so focused on new logo acquisition and action at the TOF that we can forget about the opportunity within our existing client base. But you need to do both.

The Revenue Engine framework recommends spending your time in each funnel by prioritizing the nurture funnel.

The work you do in these funnels is the heart and soul of your effort. And this chapter addresses the most complicated, most tech-intensive, and in many ways the most important funnel—the nurture funnel. You're a marketer, right? This is what you signed up to do. You signed up to *own* this nurture funnel. You signed up to tell interested humans more about your company and more about your product in a way that makes them want to buy. The job is to take people who are no longer strangers and turn them into qualified prospects.

How do you do that?

- Get clear on the ICP. This ICP iteration in your nurture funnel should be tighter than your initial broad-stroke ICP. Those ICPs that now need to get segmented into types, verticals, products, etc. Find a way that works for you to segment the group of ICPs and personas, then tie that matrix to a content calendar.

- Track the buying signals against this group of prospects. Do not let them go more than thirty days without hearing from you with more good news, ideally good news that is specific to them.

- Follow up. Enough said.

A funnel goes one way. Down. This is true in real life and in your marketing sales funnels.

Mathematically, in any CRM, moving records backward in a funnel will create havoc in your reporting. This is important to keep in mind as you watch the customer journey. The physical tech tools, like HubSpot and Salesforce we use to manage this process are "point in time" systems. Meaning the tools are collecting and reporting on data one point in time, at a time. If a record has become a lead and has made it into the sales team's hands but is not yet ready for a demo or to be "qualified" for sales, you cannot just move them back up the funnel. They must be "disqualified out" and start again from the top.

Gravity counts. Gravity matters.

The solution we often see unsophisticated sales and marketing leaders deploy is to just "create more stages!" I've seen sales and marketing funnels that look like a thousand-rung ladder with stages like "on hold," "waiting for a reply," and "finding economic buyer." In my professional opinion, these add-on stages show a misalignment between sales and marketing. Either they are using more stages to cover up the errors in the prospecting engine or a GTM strategy is missing entirely. You should have a clear ICP, know your TAM, disqualify along the way, generate and deliver content to those individuals whose problems you can solve to move them through your funnels. There's no reason to try and move accounts back up a funnel, re-nurture, or to add layers to an already pretty complicated system.

Your well-researched ICP + TAM accounts with a behavior score that clearly shows they are in market should be delivered to a sales team ready to pick up the ball and run it to the end zone.

TRACKING IN THE FUNNELS

We now know that we track human activity in the prospect funnel to see if there's any awareness in a company before that company, and all the humans associated with it, is included in the flexion point to the nurture funnel. Once that account arrives in the nurture funnel, we must track it as a *company*.

Companies are what matter in the nurture funnel because companies buy from companies in B2B.

Contacts, or humans, may enter the nurture funnel, but companies are what move through the nurture funnel to become customers. This is why the best practice is to track company activity in your reports.

The top of the nurture funnel is where we start the dossier or company profile that will feed the sales team what they need to have meaningful interactions with prospects. When a new prospect arrives at the top of the nurture funnel, otherwise known as a marketing qualified lead (MQL), it's your cue to conduct more intensive research. You'll need to reconfirm the company is an ICP and start to understand the buying committee. The average buying committee is seven to ten people in a single company. In my experience the committee gets bigger the higher up market you go.

I highly recommend you sit down with your sales leadership and even executive leadership and ask the right questions about the nurture funnel. What do they want to know, see, be involved in? When are the executives going to get involved in closing deals? How can you use the math you'll pull from this funnel for more interesting campaigns or new tech?

That's how you'll get—and keep—a seat at the table.

NURTURE CAMPAIGNS AND BEST PRACTICES

Let's consider a hypothetical. Imagine the first flexion point has been reached and these once-strangers have moved over to the nurture funnel. Now you're sharing targeted good news with them to help them get educated about the problem you solve. Applying our dating metaphor here, your nurture candidate is now eating your home-cooked meals and taking long-weekend trips with you.

We are at the top of the nurture funnel. This is the part of the customer journey where the content you're serving is highly specific and educational. Maybe you are making sure that a business development representative reaches out to the potential client you are nurturing to set up a meeting at an upcoming trade show. You might be asking if they are happy with their current software provider or for an opportunity to show them your software.

This is where you are, in a way, using Donald Miller's example of asking them to marry you over and over and over again. Your efforts equate to leaving the church reservation receipt on your fridge, then taping it to the bathroom mirror, and then putting it on the TV remote. You are trying to get their attention.

Content and campaigns developed and shared with companies and contacts in the nurture funnel should be more targeted than your prospect campaigns. I can't stress this enough: a nurture campaign starts with a list of accounts that fit specific criterion and have a specific pain point.

THE ELEMENTS OF A GREAT CAMPAIGN

CAMPAIGN STRUCTURE

SHARE GOOD NEWS	TRACK INTEREST	FOLLOW UP
• Analyst Report • Press Release • Executive Byline • LinkedIn Sponsored Executive Leadership Post • Google Paid Ads • ABM Orchestration • Blog Post/Landing Page	• Email Campaign to ICP List • Landing Pages for Traffic Driven • ABM Intent Signals of Target Segment	• SDR Follow Up Calls to Any New Interested ICP • Sales Engage Any Existing Target Account

The messaging, graphic elements, videos, etc. are important in campaign building, but as I said at the beginning of this book, I'm not a branding marketer, and there are lots of resources on copywriting and specifics written by experts in those fields. My favorite author on this topic is Robert Cialdini; his body of work on influence has influenced even this hardened math-based marketer. (See what I did there?) Instead we are going to talk about elements of a campaign that are not design related.

Campaigns that you deploy should 100 percent, always and forever, avoid RAOM. Each campaign should have a clear purpose, goal, and execution plan. You can take a stab at creating and executing those yourself, but I advise strongly against it. Instead, get alignment on and buy-in from leadership and your sales partners on how you are engaging the market. You'll create a campaign brief and use it when asking for their feedback.

Your campaign brief should have these elements:

1. Campaign Title: What you're going to call it internally when you report on your success.

2. Clearly Defined Campaign Purpose and Focus Areas: The high-level goals that tie back to your company's value proposition and ICP.

3. Campaign Objectives: We like to see three total objectives or goals. Extra points for you if they're measurable goals.

4. Campaign Strategy: The assets and deliverables you're going to use to execute this campaign.

5. Messaging Framework: The channels you're using to get this campaign out.

The example campaign gives you an idea of what good looks like in a campaign brief.

EXAMPLE CAMPAIGN

CAMPAIGN TITLE	HOW TO BUILD & MAINTAIN CARRIER RELATIONSHIPS
CAMPAIGN PURPOSE & FOCUS AREAS	To drive interest, awareness, and education amongst FTL brokers as they look to build and maintain their carrier relationships. Customers are important, but Carriers are vital. Aim to become the authoritive expert in how brokers can build and maintain strong and valuable carrier relationships.
OBJECTIVES	**Core Objective #1:** Drive leads via educational thought leadership and supporting digital channels **Core Objective #2:** Identify yourself as the authority in this market **Core Objective #3:** Audit and determine any current HubSpot workflow needs
CAMPAIGN STRATEGY	**Build integrated email + blog + social campaign directing attention to anchor whitepaper**
MESSAGING FRAMEWORK	**Digital Engagement** This integrated marketing campaign will consist of an omni-channel approach targeted across identified channels to build full funnel engagement across the total addressable market. / **Share the Voice** Utilizing the PR engine, we will amplify messaging and moments via bylines and other in-market activity, directing the same story focused on Carrier Relationships.

From there, the content elements of a great campaign are broken down into four pieces: owned, earned, shared, and paid. These elements come directly from your campaign brief, which was generated from the alignment and buy-in you secured earlier.

CAMPAIGN FRAMEWORK

OWNED (Landing Page, Website, Blog, etc.)	EARNED (PR, Executive Thought Leadership, etc.)	SHARED (Organic Social, Co-Marketing, etc.)	PAID (SEO, Paid Social, Podcast, etc.)
Anchor White Paper (gated) discussing tips for building and maintaining vendor relationships • Landing page to outline the key learnings of the White Paper, the benefits to reading and additional recommended reading (blogs or other assets) **Accessory Blog Content** • Blog 1 Vendor Relationships • Blog 2 Best Practices • Blog 3 Tech for Vendor Management	**Bylines:** Vendor Relationships Key to Combating Fraud **California Vendor Relations:** • Friends to the Vendors as they Navigate Legislation • Byline based on white paper **Media Partner:** Check Call - Vendor Relationships Key to Combating Fraud **Testimonial:** Customer's impact on their vendor relationships **Vendor Advisory Board:** Select group of Partners within our customer network to provide data on vendor growth/decline **Press release**	**Social x6** • Social 1 CTA: Anchor White Paper • Social 2 CTA: Blog 1 • Social 3 CTA: Testimonial • Social 4 CTA: Blog 2 • Social 5 CTA: Anchor White Paper • Social 6 CTA: Blog 3 **Email x3** • Email 1 CTA: Anchor White Paper • Email 2 CTA: Anchor White Paper • Email 3 CTA: Blogs 1-3	**Paid Linkedin CTA:** Boost social posts **Podcast Partner:** 30 minute interviews with customer **Paid Magazine Sponsorship:** Budget for banners **Trade Show Sponsorship:** Sponsor packages for targeted show

TRADE SHOW FOLLOW-UP

I love a good face-to-face opportunity. Trade shows and conferences are an excellent opportunity to nurture, especially if you are in a very niche market. Unfortunately we've seen more than one trade show opportunity squandered by misaligned sales and marketing teams spending lots of money without a plan.

First things first, to make attending a trade show or conference worth your time, money, and energy, you need to do your prep work. You should know who's going to be there. As an attendee or exhibitor, you should have access to a nice, tight list of who is exhibiting, then identify your ICP, and pull the records for exhibitors and attendees. It's like knowing who is going to be at the party before it starts.

Next you should have predetermined targets for your team who is attending. Before the show, for example, send three preshow emails and then work with the sales team to hyper-target the individuals you know will be at the show and who are inside the nurture funnel. You'll target them not only because they will be there, but also because you know they fit your ICP. These are the humans you want to meet at the show, selected from your nurture funnel, who you'll target in advance of the trade show or conference.

You can have the best, cleanest list in the world, have solid meetings set and attended, and have the most persuasive, charming sales team in the world, but it won't matter if there's no post-show follow-up.

Post trade show, no more than five records should be assigned to a sales rep to follow up on immediately. Asking the sales team to follow up on more than five from one show is a recipe for disaster. I cannot tell you the number of times we have done trade show work for clients only to find out that the people that were supposed to follow up on post trade show emails were so busy that they never followed up.

Without follow-up you can have hundreds of thousands, even millions of dollars in opportunity lost. Literally money just left on the table for someone else to scoop up. These wasted opportunities could have become something real, but the sales team just simply cannot handle the volume of follow-ups required to be effective. The best practice is for the sales team to take their five follow-ups and let marketing nurture the rest.

If you think it's tough to get sales teams to follow up after a show, it's even worse with executives. We almost never see regular trade show follow-up by the C-suite unless they include someone else to help them. They're so busy that very few C-suite execs ever even update the CRM.

The way we target, focus, and handle trade shows is just one perfect example of the tactics of the Revenue Engine framework. Most of our new clients simply don't have the post-show trade show follow-up buttoned up.

Instead it often looks like this: sales follows up with the people they met. The executives take two or three of those, send them an email, and then everything sort of goes back to normal. One or two deals from the show may get closed, covering the costs for the effort and making everyone happy. But if you have a methodical approach to trade show follow-up, you can crush trade shows and prove ROI. And I can tell you, everyone's way happier when that happens.

SPLITTING THE NURTURE FUNNEL

Marketing has owned everything up to this point in our framework. This includes sharing good news, clearly defining the ICP, understanding the TAM, acquiring records, and tracking interest against records and companies. It's all been marketing serving the Revenue Engine.

Now it's time to get the sales team involved.

Every company is different, but somewhere in your nurture funnel you'll "hand off" leads to the sales team.

Traditionally this is when a prospect, an MQL, is handed off to sales to qualify as an SQL to close. It's a natural handoff when this happens, and the flexion point is easy to articulate. Marketing hands off MQLs to become SQLs and measuring this handoff success seems natural. I don't disagree.

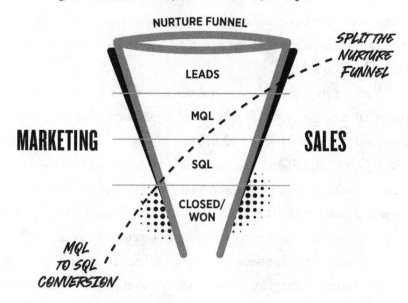

From a tech perspective, if you're using a separate marketing automation system from a CRM, a tech split will be created. An example is using HubSpot for your marketing automation and Salesforce for your CRM. Marketing owns HubSpot and qualifying. When the SQL is created, the record is moved into Salesforce.com for the sales team to own.

In this instance, HubSpot is pumping fresh gasoline into the top of the nurture funnel engine. Once an opportunity is created, Salesforce picks it up.

Inside a single tech install, just HubSpot for example, the records don't change tools, so the customer journey is easier to track (more on that in Part III). This is when a clearly defined handoff to the sales team is needed. It's usually accomplished through ownership and lead status changes.

LET'S GET REAL ABOUT EXPECTATIONS

I have seen more companies get into very serious trouble by over-promising what their marketing team is capable of, putting insane expectations on them.

Here's a hypothetical from my vertical: You want to sell a transportation management software system to shippers. You have twenty thousand businesses over $100 million in revenue that ship in your TAM. Out of your TAM, you disqualify the ones that own their own transportation management software, which reduces that twenty thousand number by half. Then you narrow it down to the ones that are going to change their transportation management software this year.

That number is just sixty. We know this because we've been doing transportation management software marketing for fifteen years. Intent data and our account-based intent software confirm there are about sixty accounts in the market appropriate to market to. In this hypothetical, the company that we are working for knows the number is sixty and yet the board tells their chief marketing officer that she is responsible for delivering forty-five MQLs *a month*. Talk about misaligned expectations.

Do the math. It is literally impossible to accomplish this. We could not help them. As consultants we need to know when expectations are impossible too—even though I am often called in to work miracles. When the leadership sets these unrealistic expectations, they are setting everyone up for failure.

Instead of spamming and blasting the marketplace trying to get 540 MQLs for some board member who picked that number out of thin air, it is important to speak frankly—and come armed with data. There are intent tools like DemandBase, 6sense, and Propensity which will tell you how many clients are in market. ZoomInfo will tell you what your actual TAM is. SalesIntel will tell you how many of those that are in your TAM are actually buying something you want to sell. The tools are out there to set realistic goals. But you must have an informed point of view. And you have to verbalize it.

CREATING ALIGNMENT

Sales and marketing must have alignment. Leaders should be doing everything in their power to try to ensure that. At the same time, marketers should be understanding it is part of their job to care about sales.

Misalignment occurs for a variety of reasons. For example, sales may kick your leads back because you are handing them prospect leads that are really still records. Maybe you've set the awareness bar too low. The first time someone shows any level of awareness, do not stick a salesperson on them.

More than once my company has been brought in to bridge the gap between the MQL and sales *just* making the first dial. We no longer do this. We no longer make the first dial in a silo because whatever list we are given is very often *not* qualified leads. We have taken "qualified" lists from marketers only to find out the people we were calling were floral shops or dry cleaners. They didn't know or care who the company was. If you've done this, you've created the misalignment because you are wasting the sales team's time. The reason they think your leads are garbage is because you are not qualifying these leads to a point where they can actually matriculate into deals. Forget a seat at the table. You could get escorted to the door on your way out.

A demand gen marketer is asking these questions to find your alignment: Are we going after volume? How many do we really need? What size deals should we be pursuing?

Navigating through the intricate paths of the prospect, nurture, and customer funnels is akin to orchestrating a complex symphony. Each funnel has its unique rhythm and role in the grand scheme of the marketing strategy. The prospect funnel lays the groundwork, the nurture funnel builds and strengthens the relationship, and the customer funnel capitalizes on the established trust to expand and deepen the business engagement.

This journey, though fraught with challenges, offers immense opportunities for businesses to connect, engage, and grow. By mastering the art of moving through these funnels with strategic intent and clarity, businesses can transform prospects into loyal customers and fuel the growth engine of their enterprise. As we close this chapter, it's clear that the nurture funnel, with its intricate nuances, stands as a testament to the transformative power of tailored marketing in the B2B market. As Vajre and Spett say: "B2B lends itself to impressive personalization, especially in contrast to the traditional approach most companies experience."[32]

REVENUE ENGINE RECAP

OK. You now know not to commit RAOM. You've also been introduced to the nuances of the nurture funnel, which is the second of three funnels in the Revenue Engine framework. Let's approach this recap a little differently from the chapters we've done so far.

Consider each key point that was covered in this chapter. Then answer the accompanying question. Feel free to write in the margins with your notes! Of course, if you were planning on sharing this book, I'd still encourage you to write in the margins if you need to. Then go pick up another copy of *The Revenue Engine* to gift to a fellow marketer. Be selfish! This copy is yours.

Key points covered in the chapter:

- The nurture funnel is where targeted content is shared with leads to educate them about the problem the company solves. Does your marketing content deliberately address your customers' pain points and clearly show how your company solves them? Do you know your customers well enough to be able to identify their problems?

- Funnels only move in one direction: down. Do you try to move back up the funnels? If so, how's that been working for you?

- In the nurture funnel, it's crucial to track company activity rather than individual contacts, as companies buy from companies in B2B. What are you doing to ensure you and your marketing team are tracking companies rather than individuals? What is the SOP when individuals at companies leave? Do you have one?

- Examples of nurture campaigns include targeted content, pre-trade show outreach, and post-trade show follow-up. Are you tracking your pre-show and post-show outreach and follow-up? How are each performing? Be honest, are you even doing that outreach and follow-up? The nurture funnel is typically split between marketing and sales, with a handoff occurring when marketing qualified leads (MQLs) become sales qualified leads (SQLs). What does your handoff look like? Is there an agreed upon trigger for it to occur? What would it take to create a handoff at your organization if there currently isn't one in place?

- Setting realistic expectations for the number of MQLs that can be generated is essential to avoid misalignment between marketing and sales teams. Moment of truth here. Are you insisting on realistic expectations from all teams? Or are you accepting unattainable goals set by people who aren't in the day-to-day trenches with you? What would it take for you to ensure alignment around realistic expectations between the marketing and sales teams?

- Did I mention the importance of follow-up? I did. Are you making sure it's being done by relevant parties? If so, what does that look like?

You've nurtured your leads to this point. They want to buy. They are at the bottom of your nurture funnel, and you are ready to move them to the top of your customer funnel. Now, at last, you can ask this once-stranger for money.

CHAPTER 6

THE CUSTOMER FUNNEL

THE BEST UPSELLING DOES NOT FEEL LIKE UPSELLING. IT FEELS LIKE MAKING THINGS BETTER FOR THE CUSTOMER.

—DANIEL H. PINK

At last! You've delivered a qualified prospect to the sales team, they closed it, and now you have a new customer!

Get excited but don't start the celebrations too early. The work isn't done. In fact, it's just the beginning of the often-overlooked customer funnel and the strategic cross-selling and upselling opportunities ahead. This is the crucial next phase in the B2B GTM journey where you build long-term relationships and unlock the true potential for sustainable growth.

This chapter explores how to maximize the value of your existing customer base. We'll cover:

- Strategies for effective cross selling and upselling, focusing on providing genuine value.

- The critical roles of customer success and account management in fostering long-lasting relationships.

- Harnessing the power of customer feedback to drive meaningful growth.

- Aligning your GTM team around a customer-centric vision for exceptional experiences.

- Key metrics to track success within the customer funnel.

- The revenue operations engine that keeps everything running smoothly.

By the end of this chapter, you'll have the knowledge and strategies to help you deepen existing relationships and understand evolving business needs. So let's embrace the multifaceted nature of the customer funnel and commit to maximizing the value of your customer base, a vital yet often underestimated component in the B2B landscape.

In other words, it's time to book the church!

STRATEGIES FOR EFFECTIVE CROSS SELLING AND UPSELLING

There is an art to cross selling and upselling that lies at the heart of maximizing customer value. The first step involves meticulously identifying opportunities within your existing customer base. You'll need to dive deep into customer purchase histories, preferences, and engagement patterns. Analyzing this data will reveal any gaps in their current solutions where your additional products or services can fit. For instance, a customer using only one mode of transportation or one piece of software may benefit from an additional mode or a new feature set. You're looking for and finding those synergistic opportunities where the customer's unmet needs align with your extended offerings.

We talk a lot about "share of wallet" with our customers in supply chain. The share of wallet concept is crucial because—spoiler alert—there is no new freight. If you are going to grow in supply chain and transportation, you are taking the work from someone else.

Share of wallet is about understanding your customer's total spend in your category and strategizing how to capture a larger portion of that spend. No shipper is going to use a single vendor globally. However, with an understanding of how *much* of the wallet you own (your share of wallet), you can identify how much opportunity is left to capture.

Making this identification requires a thorough understanding of your customer's business, challenges, and goals. This is where account management, sometimes called customer success, comes in.

THE ROLE OF CUSTOMER SUCCESS

The account management team, sometimes called customer success in SaaS environments, is responsible for the customer experience. Account managers act as the primary point of contact for customers, ensuring that their needs and expectations are consistently met. They need to understand customers' business objectives and how your offerings can help achieve them, on top of addressing customer queries and navigating challenges.

Most best-in-class companies have dedicated account managers for their biggest customers. These companies know personalized and attentive service fosters trust and loyalty. It also makes the account management team your best friend when it comes to cross selling and upselling.

The account management team's deep understanding of each customer's business, gained through ongoing often daily interactions, positions the account manager to easily identify upsell and cross-sell opportunities that align closely with the customer's evolving needs. Thanks to the account management team, you'll have a better understanding of how customers see you and where your relationship stands. You want—no, you need—your relationship with the account management team to be "sticky."

"Sticky" relationships in marketing and sales refer to how strong and lasting the connection is between a company and its customers. The stickiest relationships are ones with high customer loyalty, repeat business, and a strong, unwavering preference for the company's products or services. Basically if you and your customer have a sticky relationship, you know that customer is less likely to switch to a competitor and more likely to recommend your company to others.

The three-by-three stickiness score is one of my favorite exercises used to identify and measure just how "sticky" your relationship is with your customers.

There are ways to do this for SaaS-based companies that include frequency of use, diversity of features used, and depth of usage. But most of my clients are not SaaS, and frankly there're enough books out there for the tech community. We're focused on the not-as-sexy-to-some B2B community.

More specifically your three-by-three stickiness score measures your depth of relationship with the three layers of management inside your customer. For example, these layers could have an executive at the first level, a leader at the second, and an individual contributor at the third level.

3X3 STICKINESS

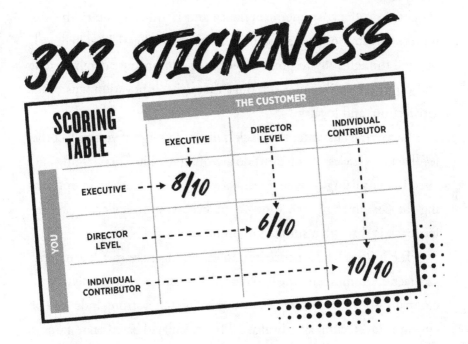

SCORING TABLE	THE CUSTOMER		
	EXECUTIVE	DIRECTOR LEVEL	INDIVIDUAL CONTRIBUTOR
EXECUTIVE	8/10		
DIRECTOR LEVEL		6/10	
INDIVIDUAL CONTRIBUTOR			10/10

Each of these relationships is given a score of one to ten, with a higher score indicating greater engagement and healthy relationships. Review these stickiness scores at least quarterly for the top 20 percent of your clients.

The three-by-three stickiness score is a valuable tool in the customer funnel, revealing clear opportunities for improvement and meaningful, actionable insights about how and where to offer new products or services.

THE POWER OF CUSTOMER FEEDBACK

Along with a strong three-by-three stickiness score, customer feedback is a powerful asset in enhancing the customer funnel. Feedback, when actively encouraged and strategically utilized, can provide invaluable insights into the customer experience and is a direct line to the customer's perceptions and expectations. Businesses that deliberately seek out and thoughtfully respond to feedback demonstrate commitment and can more easily tailor offerings that drive innovation, customer satisfaction, and loyalty.

Gathering customer feedback is like follow-up. If you collect the feedback, it's useless if you don't do anything with it. Encouraging and effectively utilizing customer feedback is a crucial strategy in optimizing the customer funnel. One of the best ways to collect customer feedback is through a simple net promoter score (NPS).

The NPS is a key metric in understanding customer loyalty and satisfaction. It measures the likelihood of a customer recommending a company's product or service to others, which is a strong indicator of customer satisfaction and loyalty. NPS is calculated based on responses to a single question: "On a scale of zero to ten, how likely are you to recommend our company/product/service to a friend or colleague?" Based on their rating, customers are categorized as promoters, passives, or detractors.

This simple yet powerful tool helps businesses gauge the overall perception of their brand and customer loyalty. Easy to execute and track, regularly tracking the NPS can provide insights into the effectiveness of the customer funnel strategies and highlight areas for improvement. By addressing the concerns of detractors and nurturing the promoters, you can have a strategic seat at the table when delivering the math around the NPS quarterly.

Also, NPS score emails can be automated in any marketing automation engine, so you have real math to share with account management leadership. That seat at the table is getting closer and closer.

ALIGNING THE GTM TEAM ON THE CUSTOMER FUNNEL

As we shared earlier in the book, the combined sales, marketing, and customer success/account management teams is a GTM team. The alignment of the GTM team ensures that everyone is working toward common goals and strategies within the customer funnel.

By establishing shared objectives, such as customer lifetime value or customer satisfaction scores, the whole GTM team can work together to develop cohesive strategies to ensure insights and feedback are regularly exchanged. No one should be operating in a vacuum.

Collaboration starts with shared access to data and insights about customer interactions, preferences, and feedback. Jointly developed customer personas and journey maps can guide the whole GTM team in creating tailored marketing materials and sales pitches. Furthermore, involving sales insights in the creation of content ensures that marketing materials address customer pain points. This way marketing can equip sales with the right assets and content to nurture leads more effectively.

MEASURING SUCCESS IN THE CUSTOMER FUNNEL

Keep in mind, "CROs all have a revenue goal we need to meet, and we work backward from that number to develop our strategy."[33]

Measuring the success of the customer funnel is essential for ensuring its effectiveness and identifying areas for improvement. Key metrics and performance indicators include customer lifetime value (CLV), customer retention rates, NPS, and conversion rates between funnel stages.

In terms of developing your strategy, Vajre says, "The most important thing to do first is to define what engagement means to you and your organization and get consensus from your leadership team. It might take many iterations to find the one that works for your business."[34]

Metrics like upsell and cross-sell rates, along with customer satisfaction scores, offer insights into the depth and quality of customer relationships—your "stickiness." Tracking these metrics over time provides valuable data on funnel performance and highlights areas needing adjustment. Since customer needs and market conditions are rapidly ever changing, you need to be continually improving and adapting. Regularly analyzing performance data enables sales and marketing teams to make data-driven decisions, ensuring the customer funnel remains dynamic and responsive to both customer and business needs.

REVENUE ENGINE RECAP

We are at the halfway point in the book! It's time to test your memory. Grab a pencil or highlighter. If there's anything in this recap that's unclear or you don't quite recall reading about it, make a note. You'll want to go back through the previous chapters and brush up before heading into Part III.

Now let's review the parts we've covered of our now thriving Revenue Engine.

We start with sharing good news.

Next we track interest.

Then we follow up.

Sounds simple enough, but the devil is in the details. Or in our case, it's in the framework and the funnels.

We started with the biggest TAM as the fuel for our *prospecting funnel*. But then we began the process of *disqualifying*. We use the prospecting funnel to track interest and qualify ICPs until those at the bottom of the funnel reach the flexion point to be an MQL. The magic is in the deltas, remember?

At the flexion point, the lead goes to the top of the *nurture funnel*. It is in this funnel that a transition is made at some point from marketing to sales. At the bottom of that funnel, there is an actual "buy." So far you've made the smart decision to not only not commit RAOM, you're also not asking strangers for money. But now they are no longer strangers, and when they want to give you money, they move to the top of the third, or *customer funnel*.

The customer funnel is not just a concluding phase in the B2B marketing journey, but rather it is a launching pad for sustainable growth and long-term customer loyalty. By focusing on deepening relationships, understanding customer needs, and effectively leveraging data, businesses can unlock the full potential of their existing customer base. This funnel, therefore, demands as much attention and strategic planning as the initial stages of attracting and nurturing leads. By mastering the customer funnel, businesses ensure a steady growth trajectory, underscored by strong, lasting customer relationships.

OK. How many things did you underline or highlight?

In Part III it's the moment of truth—time for a math lesson. Now for those of you dry-heaving, don't worry. I've brought you this far. I'm not going to kill you with calculus. But I *am* going to give you a primer on the math that will get you a seat at the leadership table.

It will not be intimidating, and I promise you that you can do it, even if you were a poli-sci major like me.

Part III will introduce you to the Revenue Engine's three Vs: Volume, Velocity, and Value.

You'll learn how each of these works, how they can be measured, and how they can transform the way you market. If you get these down pat, your Revenue Engine will be fully fired up and ready to turn over and hit the highway.

Top down, tunes up. Fuzzy dice from the rearview mirror.

PART III

MEASURING THE THREE VS: VOLUME, VELOCITY, AND VALUE

So you've made it to Part III, and you're ready to learn about the Revenue Engine's three Vs of B2B GTM measurement: volume, velocity, and value.

There are a few reasons why the GTM team needs to be responsible for measuring, creating the reports, and sharing the math around GTM activities.

1. If you want a seat at the table, you need to show a command of business and unit economics. Asking the right questions to inform your analysis will show leadership that you understand the business beyond the words and pictures that go onto the website.

2. Leadership needs to see the "so what" behind the effort and budget spent on GTM functions. I've seen too many leadership teams tell me with pride, "We don't spend money on marketing." That is ridiculous. Those who are winning are the ones executing strategic spend on the *right* GTM efforts.

3. Knowing the impact of your GTM efforts will help empower you to ask for more budget on the efforts that work. Plus, measuring helps you decide quickly what isn't working. Fail fast and keep testing.

4. Every leadership team says they want to make data-driven decisions. However, most companies are still run by someone's gut (I say this with confidence). "Scale" is a sexy word, but the math behind that scale is often elusive.

Having said all that, here's an example of how and why this can go wrong. We were invited to reply to an RFP for a well-known enterprise company in supply chain. "Great," I thought, "These are sophisticated marketers who know what they're doing. They have an RFP." Except through the course of the diligence period we came to understand what they were asking for. Actual numbers have been changed to protect the innocent. Here's what we learned:

Year 1: Their pipeline target was $20 million and revenue target was $10 million. They missed both targets by 50 percent. So their year-end actuals were $10 million in pipeline and $5 million in closed revenue. The leadership was looking for more lead gen to fuel their sales team.

Year 2: This is the year they wanted to hire us to help. Their goal was to increase the pipeline from year one to year three by 5(x). The new goal was $100 million and $50 million in closed deals.

This math just doesn't add up. A 5x improved return in two years with no major changes in strategy or spend would be setting ourselves up for dramatic failure. Needless to say we chose not to work with this company (and ultimately end up being the whipping boy when it didn't work).

My point is this math seems elusive for even the most sophisticated. Show up with a point of view and you can win a seat at the table.

Before we move on, I'll tell you a story that illustrates a little about what's involved—and then do some math. (By the way, this is a true story.)

I got fired from being Girl Scout Cookie Mom.

And (by now you expect no less of me), of course, I can spin this into a lesson on the three Vs.

My fall from grace as Cookie Mom started off with me having the best of intentions. I was (and am) a busy mom, CEO, entrepreneur, wife, a doer of "all the things," when the new Girl Scout troop at my kids' school asked for volunteers. Clearly I could not be the troop leader—I can't be at school every other Tuesday at two in the afternoon. It's just not an option for me as someone with too many plates to spin. But I could volunteer for a twelve-week project as the Cookie Mom. I thought to myself, "I run projects all the time. This is what I do for a living. Yes! I can definitely run the cookies project for twelve weeks. How hard can it be?"

You see where this is going.

All my friends who have kids older than mine offered me this urgent advice: "Don't! The worst thing is Cookie Mom. Don't be Cookie Mom." But I was a combination of cocky and naive. I thought, "Running cookies sales is just *logistics*. I got this."

Thus, on Cookie Mom night, where I gathered with all the other Cookie Moms at a local church, we were told we could sell cookies online for the first time. The entrepreneur in me thought, "This is great." Our girls would get a special badge for driving e-commerce sales. Not only that, for security reasons, our kids wouldn't even have to send any emails. Instead, we parents would simply provide the email addresses, and the Girl Scouts would send out the emails on their behalf.

I was informed that if a Girl Scout sent out thirty emails, she would earn a badge. That's adorable. I had a higher *volume* in mind.

I asked, "What is the badge when she sends thirty thousand emails?" I thought this was a reasonable question, but the Girl Scout leadership looked at me kind of cross-eyed, and asked, "Does your daughter know thirty thousand people?"

I replied, "No, but I send emails for a living, and if you're telling me that these are going to come anonymously from the Girl Scout server, I will send you thirty thousand emails and watch my daughter crush it on a passive income for her Girl Scout troop." Eyes popped.

Here was a volume, velocity, and value problem if ever I saw one. The Girl Scouts, unfortunately, did not see it that way and informed me that was not the "spirit" of cookie sales.

Frankly I thought it showed ingenuity. I was *engineering the revenue* of the Girl Scout troop. I calculated that I knew my volume and value would amount to a thousand boxes sold. I might even add Google advertising, Facebook, Instagram! Again I got cross-eyed looks. *Why on earth would you do Facebook advertising for Girl Scouts?* Why? Because everyone loves Thin Mints!

I was on fire. Girl Scout fire. Next it was time for some velocity. I ran that ship like I would run any project. I held Zoom calls. I had an Asana board, I had bullet-pointed emails, PowerPoint decks. I was killin' it (or so I thought!).

Fast-forward to about week ten. It's Girl Scout cookie pickup time, which is the most stressful part about cookie logistics because you go from digital stuff happening to physically driving to a place and doing the manual labor of picking and packing all these cookies. Of course, this is still *logistics*. I'm sending emails. I'm organizing. I've got this down.

I am a Girl Scout Cookie Revenue Engine Machine. Until I'm not.

Alas, one of the moms does not appreciate the way that I'm organizing Girl Scout cookie pickup. She says she feels like she is my employee. And she tells me, "I feel like you are talking to us as if we work for you." In my head I thought, *Well, technically, in a way you do, for these twelve weeks. Technically I'm the project manager.* I am not sure that response was appreciated.

Well, I woke up one morning ready to do my two hours of Girl Scout Cookie Mom work, and I could not log into the portal. Yup. I had been passive-aggressively fired as Cookie Mom.

One of my personal friends is on the board of Girl Scouts in my region. After helping me reestablish my Cookie Mom job, she said the obligatory: "I told you so. The Cookie Mom job is the worst!"

But we crushed our cookie goal. My daughter sold the most cookies, and it was amazing. I *was* unceremoniously fired for being too direct in my Girl Scout Cookie Mom approach—however, we did sell about two thousand boxes online (volume)! Passive income for the win. Funny enough, they asked me to come back the next year. (Don't worry, I knew better.)

One more thing. I know I've hammered home that you can't ask strangers for money. The one exception is the Girl Scouts because everyone loves a Girl Scout cookie.

While this has been a playful example, we're actually going to go over some math before we move on so that the next three chapters make full sense to you. I promise—it will not give you hives.

WHY THE MATH MATTERS

Let's quickly recap the Revenue Engine so far:

- You are putting out good news into the marketplace that matters to your ideal customer profile (ICP).

- You have identified your TAM, you have secured their email addresses, you know who they are, they know who you are because you know that they are in the nurture funnel.

- You have some records that are turning into prospects. We can use the word "lead" at this point in the flexion point into your nurture funnel. You are delivering well-qualified leads to sales and those leads are opening opportunities.

- You have customers who you are actively cross selling and upselling to. In other words, you have done the groundwork this book has laid out for our framework. It is all coming together.

- The engine is on; campaign management is happening. You have some media relations gears turning. Your engine should be working or at least you have what you need to turn the engine on. But harken back to our very first chapter when I told you that you cannot show up to the meeting without math.

The trap many young marketers fall into is thinking (or worse, saying out loud), "Look at all the work I'm doing. Hey, boss, look at all the campaigns we're running. Look at all the Facebook followers we have, look at all the activity, look at all the blog posts that I'm putting out."

This mindset is missing the point. The point is that the leadership team needs to see *measurable* results that impact revenue. So when we talk about measurement, we are not talking about email opens or clicks or "vanity metrics." These vanity metrics might make you feel good and look impressive on paper, but they have no relation to business outcomes or to your revenue bottom line.

VANITY VS. MEANINGFUL
METRICS

COMMON VANITY METRICS AND THEIR MORE MEANINGFUL COUNTERPARTS:

Vanity Metric: Page Views vs Meaningful Metric: Conversion Rate

Page views indicate how many times a web page was viewed, but they don't reveal how these views impact your business. Plus, Google Analytics (G4) page views are anonymous. Conversely, the meaningful metric of the conversion rate indicates the proportion of visitors who preform a targeted action, such as requesting a quote or subscribing to a newsletter, providing a direct link to business outcomes.

Vanity Metric: Number of Social Media Followers vs Meaningful Metric: Engagement Rate (Likes, Shares, Comments)

A high number of followers can be misleading if they are not actively engaging with your content. The engagement rate is a better indicator of how your audience interacts with and values your content. Knowing *WHO* is following your content is also important. There are social tools to help you measure your social audience.

Vanity Metric: Email Open Rate vs Meaningful Metric: Click-Through Rate (CTR)

While open rates show how many people open an email, they don't reflect the effectiveness of the email content. CTR, which measures how many people clicked on a link within the email, is a more direct measure of interest and engagement. Add a step of UTM coding in every link and you can start to show attribution or influence per campaign.

> **Vanity Metric:** Impressions vs Meaningful Metric: Return on Ad Spend (ROAS)
>
> Impressions tell you how many times your ad was displayed, but not its effectiveness in generating revenue. ROAS measures the revenue generated for every dollar spent on advertising, directly linking to financial performance. This can be hard to measure if you're not in e-comm, but you can have a point of view and a goal to start.
>
> **Vanity Metric:** Total Website Traffic vs Meaningful Metric: Bounce Rate and Average Session Duration
>
> High website traffic is less meaningful if visitors leave quickly. Bounce rate and average session duration provide insights into visitor quality and engagement with your site content.
>
> This is just a sample of how shifting focus from vanity metrics to these more meaningful metrics helps marketers to make data-driven decision that genuinely contribute to business growth and success.

When we discuss revenue, revenue mapping, or revenue operations, we're diving into the mathematics of the business. The leadership team wants to see metrics that answer three key questions:

- How many deals are needed to meet our goal? (Volume)

- How much does each prospect need to be worth to meet our goal? (Value)

- How quickly can we close these deals to meet our goal? (Velocity)

This isn't just about measuring campaigns; it's about a holistic approach to measurement that encompasses both the business and campaign economics.

THE THREE VS EXPLAINED

1. Volume: This refers to the count of records, leads, marketing qualified leads (MQLs), sales qualified leads (SQLs), and opportunities at a given point in time. It's a metric typically tracked over time to gauge the number of potential deals.

2. Velocity: This measures how quickly records move through the funnel stages, from top to bottom or between funnels. Tracking velocity requires a CRM with time stamp capabilities and helps identify key flexion points in the sales process.

3. Value: This indicates the worth of each deal, which is often the most visible metric and the one of greatest interest to the C-suite.

These three metrics—volume, velocity, and value—work together to provide leading indicators of how your marketing and sales strategies, campaigns, and teams are performing.

A REVENUE ENGINE MODEL

We've developed a straightforward microeconomic model to help the GTM team create meaningful measurements for the C-suite. While it may look complex, it's really just an elaborate Excel sheet. But it *is* important that you know how to use it and can explain the philosophy behind it.

MONTHLY GOALS CALCULATOR

VALUE OF ONE DEAL (ARR or LTV)	LEAD TO MQL DELTA	NUMBER OF LEADS NEEDED	MQL to SQL DELTA	NUMBER OF MQLS NEEDED	SQL TO CLOSED/WON DELTA	NUMBER OF SQL NEEDED	CLOSED/WON GOALS MONTHLY	ANNUAL GOAL
$350,000	30%	33	40%	10	50%	4	2	$7,560,000

ANNUAL GOAL

Set by your leadership team, the annual goal should consider how much of the total revenue marketing is responsible for generating or influencing. The delta, or difference, between what you think is possible and what leadership expects is your point of view.

PRODUCTS

This model can be adapted for multiple products. Most of our clients have various products or service lines. Just add another row for each product's average deal size.

AVERAGE DEAL SIZE (ANNUAL RUN RATE OR LIFETIME VALUE)

Your ARR or average deal size is *one* number, not a range. The word average is there for a reason. This value represents an average deal with your ICP. The value of deals, whether using ARR or LTV, represents how much a customer is worth to the business. Choose one metric and stick with it. For multiple products, you'll need multiple values. Normalize outliers to find an average you can use for modeling.

A note on ARR versus LTV: We build this model with our clients when we start on an engagement, and it requires a few things from leadership. It requires they *know* the ARR or LTV of the ICP. One time a client said to me, "Well, our ARR is anywhere from $30 thousand to $3 million." That is not a value, that is a range with a 100x spread. Clearly this CEO didn't know who his perfect customer was, and it was an uphill battle to help him when his go-to-market strategy changed daily—with his definition of his ICP.

NUMBER OF DEALS TO GOAL

To determine the number of deals needed to hit your goal, divide your annual goal by the average deal value.

CLOSE RATE

This *should* be an easily attainable percentage since any salesperson worth the title can rattle off their tongue how close they came to goal last month or quarter. Sophisticated sales leaders also share this number with leadership on a regular basis to help forecast. Ask, "Ms. Sales Leader, what is your average close rate?" She should tell you a percentage. It *should* be that simple. If it's not available, make it up. Close rate is the percentage in a period of time. Have a point of view by using CRM data to validate your delta.

NUMBER OF SQLS

Calculate the number of SQLs needed by multiplying the total volume of deals by the close rate. The sales team should define and report this number. The bottom of the funnel will be tricky—what counts as the stage just before the deal is closed? Contract delivered, RFP responded to, pricing delivered? It could be any number of flexion points. I would argue that this is 100 percent a sales-driven number. Again, the sales team should be reporting it back to the team.

MQL TO SQL DELTA

This is the percentage of those records that make it to the middle of the funnel (or stage MQL), then make it through to the sales team to follow up on. We're looking for the fraction of the top of funnel who regularly completes most of the sales process, even if we don't close them all. This delta is all about momentum.

NUMBER OF MQLS

Depending on your company, sales stages, sophistication of your GTM engine, etc., your MQL count could mean a lot of things. For some clients it's the first time a meeting is set, and for others it's a first opportunity to quote. Consistency is key but remain flexible as a team when defining this point. The simplest way to give this a definition is the flexion point between the prospect and nurture funnel. It's an easy number to count and *should* be an easy way to get everyone on the same page.

LEADS TO MQL DELTA

Here's where things get sexy: You are looking for the *rate of change* between the top of the funnel and the middle. This rate measures the transition from the top-of-funnel leads to middle-of-funnel MQLs. It reflects the percentage of new records that progress through the funnel steps.

NUMBER OF LEADS NEEDED TO HIT GOAL

This is the number of top-of-funnel records you will need to hit your goal. I prefer to think of these as the fresh gas you are adding to your Revenue Engine on a regular basis. These are *records* you are tracking against in the prospect funnel.

SPOILER ALERT: 99 PERCENT OF OUR CLIENTS GUESS AT THE COUNT OF LEADS NEEDED NUMBER FOR THREE REASONS:

1. They aren't actually acquiring new ICP company or contact data, so they don't have the denominator of that equation. They've been sitting on the same database of ten thousand records for three years.

2. They don't know how or where these new records came from. Every sales rep has access to ZoomInfo to pull "leads" down like candy and send bundles of unsolicited cold email to unsuspecting victims.

3. No one has ever asked for this delta, and they have no idea where to get it.

REVENUE ENGINE RECAP

So now you have all these numbers, and you can start to set some goals. My suggestion is to *play* with the math. Yes, you read that right, *play*. Make yourself some scenarios. This book isn't about regression or sensitivity analysis of financial data, but if you have a friend in finance who can help, give it a shot.

This is the simplest form of a marketing model we could make for this book. You should be able to use it and see the volume of records you'll need at each stage of the funnel to meet the company's goals, and the value those deals need to be to make your target. This will help inform your point of view.

Once you have the model created, share it. The entire GTM team (sales, marketing, and customer success) should all agree that these are the numbers we're held accountable for hitting.

Then you just have to figure out *how*.

Go to therevenueengine.com for a downloadable template.

CHAPTER 7

THE THREE VS: VOLUME

METRICS ARE CRUCIAL IN SALES; THEY PROVIDE A CLEAR PICTURE OF PERFORMANCE AND PIPELINE HEALTH. WITHOUT MEASURING KEY ASPECTS LIKE VOLUME, VELOCITY, AND VALUE, YOU'RE NAVIGATING BLIND.

—MATTHEW DIXON AND BRENT ADAMSON, *THE CHALLENGER SALE: TAKING CONTROL OF THE CUSTOMER CONVERSATION*

Measuring volume is the driving force behind your Revenue Engine, and we're taking a close look at this powerful metric in chapter seven. While the traditional B2B sales funnel includes stage awareness, consideration, intent, evaluation, and purchase, too many marketers have a difficult time connecting these words to a prospect's actions and actions to revenue.

Measuring volume is all about:

- Quantifying the number of records, ICPs, and prospects at each funnel stage.

- Gaining a raw, numerical look at your pipeline strength and revenue potential.

- Recognizing the challenges in tracking volume and strategies to overcome them.

- Understanding the importance of cross-functional collaboration in driving volume.

- Aligning your Revenue Engine team for maximum impact.

Here's the reality: generating revenue is a cross-functional endeavor. Marketing, sales, and customer success teams must operate as a unified force, with volume as the rallying cry. Silos are the enemy, and collaboration is vital for propelling prospects through the funnel.

In this chapter, we'll explore why volume reigns supreme as a revenue catalyst. You'll gain insights into common volume measurement pitfalls and strategies to overcome them. And above all you'll understand the pivotal role volume plays in aligning your Revenue Engine for maximum impact. I know you'll appreciate the critical nature of volume more than those Cookie Moms did.

TRADITIONAL MARKETING FUNNEL

AWARENESS = LEAD

DISCOVERY = MQL

EVALUATION = SQL

INTENT = SQL

PURCHASE = CLOSED/WON

LOYALTY = CUSTOMER

A healthy funnel will have a large volume at the top that progressively narrows down toward the bottom. However, it's not just the number that matters; the rate at which prospects move from one stage to the next is also crucial. We'll get to velocity in the next chapter.

Measuring the volume of records and prospects and leads in your sales funnel serves multiple purposes.

First, it helps assess the overall health of your sales and marketing pipeline. A low volume at the top of funnel might indicate inadequate lead generation efforts, while a drop-off at a specific stage could signal a problem with how your product or service is presented or priced. By creating a model and consistently comparing your progress against it, you can identify significant discrepancies early on. Using the analogy of a Revenue Engine, it's important to consider what type of fuel (resources or inputs) is being fed into the system to keep it running efficiently.

Second, volume metrics aid in forecasting sales and revenue. By understanding the typical conversion rates at each stage of the funnel, future sales can be predicted more accurately.

Conant advises, "Looking at the amount of pipeline you've historically had at each buying stage and the revenue you've attained with those numbers, it's simply a math exercise to determine how many accounts you'll need at each buying stage in order to achieve your current revenue goals."[35]

Finally, tracking volume over time helps in identifying economic trends, and seasonal fluctuations, which are key in strategic planning.

Volume is the ideal opportunity for you, as marketer, to show the sales team how much you care. (Trust me, you want to be friends with them. I hope this has become clearer for you by now.) For me, volume is working backward from the sales goal.

In Aaron Ross's *Predictable Revenue,* he says, "To ensure alignment on pipeline generation a common language and common definitions for prospects, leads, and opportunities must be created. One of the biggest problems is usually miscommunication and misunderstandings of terms and metrics between executives and directors."[36]

With better alignment, sales teams can avoid disqualifying smaller deals simply because there is so much pressure to "just get leads in." As Ross states, there is an opportunity cost to small deals; they "waste time and resources that could be spent looking for or working on larger ones."[37]

As Conant advises, "You only want to invest your time, budget, and energy in the accounts that are a good fit and in market to buy."[38]

It boils down to a simple back-of-the-napkin calculation for demand generation: determining the number of deals we need in the pipeline to achieve our shared company goal. You must commit to and understand that it is not marketing's goal, not revenue operations' goal, but the *company's goal*. For a company to succeed, it is essential for sales and marketing to have alignment and to act as a team. If you have four people in a boat, and they're all rowing in different directions, you're going nowhere fast. Coach them to row toward a particular end in mind, and you'll get there in no time.

Conant says, "Being laser focused on where you place your bets yields much greater rewards than trying to reach every possible account."[39]

CHALLENGES IN MEASURING VOLUME

I'm not going to lie. While measuring volume is essential, it does come with challenges. The primary challenge is ensuring data accuracy and consistency. Inaccurate data can lead to misguided strategies and poor decision-making. Another challenge is the integration of different data sources. Marketing and sales often use separate tools, making it difficult to get a unified view of the funnel. Overcoming these challenges requires a commitment to data hygiene and the integration of marketing and sales platforms.

Your first question when you begin trying to measure volume should be: What are the company's goals? If you do not know what the goal is, you have a serious problem. The marketer must be aware of the revenue goals for the year, the quarter, and other relevant time periods. Then to determine the plan for achieving those goals, they should start by assessing the top-of-funnel volume while also considering factors such as velocity and value.

I can't tell you how many young marketers I've mentored, spoken to, or interviewed who were operating in a tiny vacuum inside their company. When I ask them what their revenue goal is for the year, they look at me cross-eyed. The leadership team has goals, trust me, and if you don't know them, you'll never have a seat at the table.

BUILDING THE REVENUE ENGINE—AS A TEAM

A reminder once again: If you are not building this Revenue Engine with your sales partners, you can't win. It may seem like a game of corporate politics that we have to play. However, you can't win as a marketer, as a marketing leader, a marketing consultant, or a revenue operations consultant unless you work with the sales team and the sales leader to build volume, velocity, and value metrics. Marketing serves sales, so the goals must be set by the sales leadership and shared with marketing. If marketing operates and sets goals in a vacuum, then they will mean nothing to the sales team.

Latané Conant has said, "When revenue teams are not aligned, they inevitably (and quickly) hit a ceiling in terms of what they can accomplish."[40]

A strong, sophisticated sales leader will see the value in a strong marketing partner. A sophisticated leader is someone secure in their job, their ability to sell, and their ability to close. A strong sales leader is someone who is a learner, someone who's always searching for the best new tech, and someone who is curious about best practices and sees marketing as a partner.

In my experience, there are intelligent sales leaders, and there are closers. Sometimes they overlap. But not always.

Unfortunately, sales leadership roles are often awarded to those who can close the largest deals rather than the best managers or organizational leaders. Top performers get promoted into positions of power because of their sales abilities, not their leadership skills. Even if you, as a marketer, put up impressive attribution numbers and millions in pipeline value, an unsophisticated sales leader may be reluctant to give you credit. The lack of collaboration presents a significant obstacle. Ideally, executive leadership should set the expectation and tone of partnership between sales and marketing. However, the onus frequently falls to the more junior marketing professional to demonstrate value and establish sufficient credibility with the sales team early on to earn influence and investment in joint initiatives. It is an unfair burden, symptomatic of underlying misalignment, but often a reality nevertheless.

If you don't have a leader in a position to capitalize on the democratization of these technology tools and these strategies to get in front of customers, if you're still relying on a phone book to find prospects, if you're still back in 2006—so long, because you're not going to win. You may be fine for the next five to ten years because things still need to evolve and progress. But in the long game, you're way behind.

When marketers present concrete data, such as attrition rates, lead attribution, and millions of dollars in deals closed by the sales team, they may still struggle to receive credit for their contributions if they haven't collaborated with the sales leader from the beginning. It's crucial for marketers to work closely with the sales leaders early on, ensuring they feel invested in the work being done together. Failure to do so may result in an unsophisticated sales leader not acknowledging the marketer's efforts, which is the biggest challenge marketers face.

It's the CEO's responsibility to ensure that the sales leader is working in tandem with the marketing team and that everyone is on the same page. If there is a disconnect between the two departments, the fault lies with the CEO, as the buck stops at her desk. It is her duty to have the right sales leader in place who can effectively collaborate with the marketing team and guide them along the journey. Failing to establish this synergy falls squarely on the CEO's shoulders.

A lack of synergy usually equates to a failing company or at the very least, a lack of a repeatable revenue engine.

REVENUE MATTERS

A good amount of this book is dedicated to measurement and backing up your math. You want to be able to show your boss real math that they, in turn, can show the board. To do this well, you need to consider what the board really cares about. And what is the only thing that matters in the boardroom? *Revenue.*

You can put a bunch of fancy stuff around it. You can dress it up. You can talk about attribution modeling, you can talk about intent signals, you can talk about awareness, but at the end of the day, the entire purpose is to measure the impact on revenue.

Another item you need to deeply understand before you start measuring volume is the impact per deal or closed revenue for your company.

So as a marketer, you have to get realistic numbers from your leadership team. Once again, this might be something that you can figure out on your own. By going to leadership and asking smart questions, you'll not only get realistic numbers, but you'll also get their alignment. Start by asking, "What is our average deal size, ARR, or LTV?"

The math here needs to be very simple, but it does need to be decided on and then codified in writing. The most important thing here is that you do not move this needle.

Volume goals are not a goalpost to be moved.

Now most marketing goalposts should be moved: number of records, number of leads, how many in the pipeline. Those numbers should constantly be changing. In fact, if you are doing a good job of list hygiene, which we covered previously, those numbers *will* be changing.

I like the metrics Aaron Ross lays out in "If You Only Track Five Metrics" advice:

- New leads created per month (also from what source).

- Conversion rate of leads to opportunities.

- Number of, and pipeline dollar value of, qualified opportunities created per month. This is the most important leading indicator of revenue!

- Conversion rates of opportunities to closed deals.

- Booked revenues in three categories: New Business, Add-On Business, Renewal Business.[41]

Notice that Ross calls out three kinds of revenue due to all revenue not being equal. In our model we track new business in the nurture funnel and add on or renewal in the customer funnel.

CHANGING VOLUME

The GTM team can clearly adjust the volume of records at the TOF, or the number of strangers you are reaching on a regular basis. As you enter more records into the top of your prospecting funnel, you will want to watch this grow over time.

I've mentioned before that there are roughly twenty thousand companies with meaningful shipping volume in the US. Here is a snapshot of what taking that twenty thousand TAM and entering those records into a HubSpot actually looks like. It wasn't a one time dump because people's titles change, and we *shouldn't* be sending emails to eighty thousand email addresses at a time anyway.

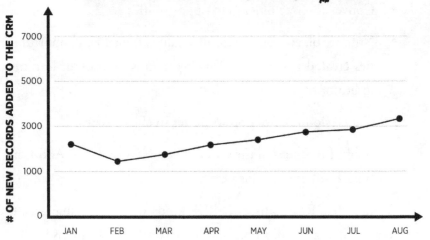

However, the number that you assign to the value of a deal in your engine *should* be static. This should be specific for at least a year. You can then put your volume goals around this value number. As Conant attests, "Being laser focused on where you place your bets yields much greater rewards than trying to reach every possible account."[42]

REVENUE ENGINE RECAP

Volume is the first of the three Vs in the Revenue Engine framework. Volume refers to the number of records, ICPs, or prospects at each stage of the funnel. Tracking volume will allow you to assess the overall health of your sales and marketing pipeline, forecast sales and revenue, and identify trends and fluctuations.

Key points covered in the chapter:

- A healthy funnel should have a large volume at the top that progressively narrows down toward the bottom.

- Measuring volume helps assess the health of the sales and marketing pipeline, forecast sales and revenue, and identify trends and fluctuations.

- Challenges in measuring volume include ensuring data accuracy and consistency, as well as integrating different data sources from marketing and sales.

- Building the Revenue Engine requires a team effort, with sales and marketing working together toward a common goal. Alignment between the two departments is crucial.

- Revenue is the primary focus in the boardroom, and marketers must understand the impact of their efforts on revenue generation.

Remember, the Revenue Engine requires the entire team. Don't operate in a vacuum. Investing time and energy in accounts that fit the ICP and the company's goals relies on strong alignment between marketing and sales teams.

All of these goals—as by now you have no doubt realized—count on alignment between marketing and sales.

As Conant says, "We agree that working more accounts is not the answer; it's all about working the right accounts."[43]

The only thing I'd add to that quote is that it's also about working *together* on the right accounts.

CHAPTER 8

THE THREE VS: VELOCITY

PROSPECTING IS THE FUEL FOR YOUR SALES ENGINE. KEEPING YOUR PIPELINE FULL ENSURES THAT YOU MAINTAIN A STEADY VELOCITY IN YOUR SALES PROCESS, WHICH IS KEY TO CONSISTENT PERFORMANCE.

—JEB BLOUNT, AUTHOR, *FANATICAL PROSPECTING*

Remember that Girl Scout cookie frenzy? How long does it take for an initial "I might want Thin Mints" to transform into a committed "Send me ten boxes"? Girl Scout velocity operates in seconds.

Velocity refers to the rate at which records, leads, and prospects move through your funnel. From initial contact to closed deal, this metric is the ultimate litmus test for your GTM engine's efficiency. It's a leading indicator of your ability to generate revenue and drive growth. A higher velocity signals a well-oiled, high-performing GTM process, empowering your sales team to convert prospects into paying customers. Remember, B2B sales cycles can be lengthy and complex.

In this chapter, we'll dive into:

- The importance of making velocity a focal point for your revenue teams.

- Tactics for testing, monitoring, and optimizing campaigns to boost velocity.

- Strategies for identifying and eliminating bottlenecks in your sales process.

- Real-world examples showcasing different "good" velocity benchmarks.

- Distinguishing pipeline velocity from sales cycle length.

- Common obstacles in measuring velocity accurately and how to overcome them.

By mastering velocity, you'll be able to close more deals in less time, creating a virtuous cycle that propels your Revenue Engine forward.

TRACKING VELOCITY

Velocity can feel elusive. Volume is easy; it's a count. Value should be simple; it's a dollar amount. Velocity can elude us; it is a rate. *Velocity is time.*

According to Conant, there are four factors of, or impacts to, velocity:[44]

1. Increase the number of new opportunities.

2. Increase average selling price.

3. Increase win rate.

4. Decrease sales cycle length.

There is only one place to get velocity in your GTM function, the CRM.

Hopefully you remember when I said that every record *should* have time-stamped activities inside the CRM. From the first time you uncovered an email address (or they handed it over freely), to the last time that record interacted with your website or a human at your company, you should have a time stamp for every interaction.

You cannot track velocity without a CRM.

And your CRM is useless if the data is inaccurate.

Big sigh. I know, I feel you. I have yet to meet a CRM and marketing automation tech stack that didn't need a little tender love and care from our revenue operations team.

A NOTE ON *REVENUE OPERATIONS*

This is a new term for what used to be the CRM administrator's job. But now the revenue operations leader and team are responsible for more than just the CRM. Their responsibilities extend into marketing automation, integrations with outside services or partners, data lakes, and business intelligence reporting tools. It can be a big job.

Smart, sophisticated revenue operators embrace motion and the momentum of AI and intent data and the democratization of intent tools, which we'll talk about in chapter ten. Your competition will eat you for lunch if you do not have a sophisticated revenue operations engine behind you. It may not be tomorrow; it may be in five or ten years. But it's coming—and a strong revenue operations engine will give you an edge.

In 2006 when I was on the floor of Echo Global Logistics, we were still using *actual phone books* literally dialing for dollars. *Actual phone books.* Salesforce.com did not exist. We didn't have a customer relationship management system.

In my (not that long) lifetime we have gone from zero technology and using phone books—"banging" the phone, dialing for dollars—to understanding the buying signals from prospects, leads, and customers with intent data. Think about your own personal shopping habits or how you approach considering working with a new company or person. Keep in mind that today, 75 percent of companies prefer rep-free sales.[45] They do their research.

Now you can see all that activity and the volume of change. We are at the nascent start of another massive shift that will change how B2B marketing and sales work (but not the Revenue Engine framework, which is timeless).

AI is new in most verticals. In my space as of this book's publication, we have not seen it proliferate operations, but just wait. I'm no AI expert, but I know we are going to see it integrated into all aspects of marketing. The data you can get from companies, small businesses, big businesses, what they're buying, how they're buying it, what the math looks like on their share of wallet, what the math looks like on their model specifics—it's all coming.

Whether you are using Salesforce, HubSpot, Zoho, or some bright and shiny new CRM that is to come down the road, you have time stamps. (Unless, for some reason, you are using Google Sheets or Excel. If you're using Google Sheets, you should definitely be using HubSpot instead!) All CRMs of any sort of credibility and reputation are time stamped.

But the time stamping also only works if three things are happening in your CRM:

1. You are *using* it.

2. Everyone (including the C-suite) is *using* it.

3. You have set up the appropriate fields to track the flexion points within and between your funnels.

FUNNEL TRACKING

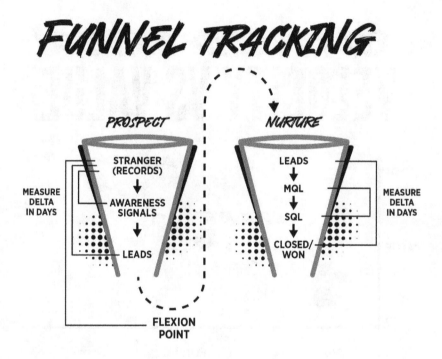

In a B2B sales environment, you are tracking the progress of companies, not individuals, through the sales funnel. Your CRM should tell you when these companies move from one stage of the funnel to the next. By tracking and reporting these movements, you can create metrics that allow you to measure performance and hold team members accountable for their contributions to the sales process.

But all velocity is not equal.

Shocking, I know. As consultants, we regularly get asked a question that is both one of my favorites and also one that can be *super* hard to answer.

"What does good look like?"

Lucky for me I operate in a very specific niche, so I usually have an answer to that question, but I often use examples to stay out of the "but you told me this would happen" dance we can get ourselves into.

There is an inverse relationship between velocity and value.

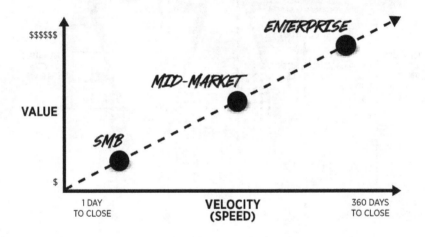

Here's an example of two companies based on real companies (but names redacted) and their pipeline and value metrics:

Company A is a transportation management software company that targets the middle and upper markets of the freight brokerage and freight-forwarding industries. Their ARR deal value is about $30,000, and they have a ninety-day implementation process. It's a SaaS product, and they take customers from their competitors often.

They use a lot of paid media and digital channels to drive prospects to a demo.

Company B is a material handling and distribution company that targets only the Fortune 50. Their deal size is $10 million ARR, and they sign three- to five-year deals that include tons of capital expenditure and planning. Often there is a discovery and planning component to their work because the risk is so high. They are the leaders in this space and have Gartner to back that up. They invest heavily in thought leadership and have a clear point of view on two verticals they are "best in class" in.

	COMPANY A	COMPANY B
VOLUME	TAM is 50,000 with a 20% Prospect to CW Conversion	TAM is 500 with a 15% Prospect to CW Conversion
VELOCITY	90 Days	12 – 18 months
VALUE	$30,000	$10,000,000

Company A will have a faster velocity to close, but they need more volume to match the value of Company B's pipeline. It takes Company A 333 deals to match the value of one deal for Company B.

Company B only needs to close a handful of deals a year to hit their goals, but they need to start the sales process twenty-four to thirty-six months before their future customers even know they have a problem.

Neither is better or more "right" than the other, but they are very different. As you are setting up expectations with your leadership team be sure to ask the really difficult questions needed to nail down your *current* velocity. Are you closer to Company A or Company B in terms of volume, velocity, and value?

OBSTACLES IN MEASURING VELOCITY

As you journey down the Yellow Brick Road of marketing math, you will inevitably be asked this question: "Can we see a month-over-month comparison?" or "Where did we start versus where we are now?" or "How do we know if we've improved?"

Unfortunately no CRM (as of this writing in 2024) will spit out month-over-month changes in velocity through your funnel in the way that your leadership team will ask for them. Certainly your leadership team will appreciate a "snapshot in time" look from HubSpot. But, most likely, they would rather see the year-over-year delta between January and January, or December and December. Unfortunately, my beleaguered marketer, that is much harder to do. That requires the use of spreadsheet software like Excel or specialized business intelligence tools such as Microsoft Power BI, Domo, or Tableau to process and visualize the data effectively.

> Business intelligence (BI) is software that ingests business data and presents it in user-friendly views such as reports, dashboards, charts, and graphs. BI tools enable business users to access different types of data—historical and current, third-party and in-house, as well as semi-structured data and unstructured data like social media. Users can analyze this information to gain insights into how the business is performing.[46]

QUICK TIP

At LeadCoverage, we recommend setting a benchmark. If you haven't already, set a benchmark right now. Today. (No seriously, go do it right now.) Pull a set of reports that have the number of records in each stage of each funnel and pop it into an excel document, or just save the PDFs of the reports for later. Do not just leave the report to languish in the CRM.

GARBAGE IN AND GARBAGE OUT

You've heard it before. This old saying can be used for nutrition and exercise as well as your CRM. Jim Collins, one of my favorite business authors, talks about "disciplined action" in his book *Good to Great*. And the same can be said for your CRM.

You cannot get great leadership-ready decision-making data if the system you're using to get that math is not clean. We've talked about some of the cleaning of lists and ICPs and personas earlier in the book, but this challenge is more political than anything.

The C-suite is probably talking to prospects occasionally. And they're definitely not logging it in the CRM.

It's one of the hardest problems to solve on the GTM team. Most C-suite leaders are moving a million miles a minute, making decision after decision, and they don't have the time and energy (nor should they be spending time and energy on) to update the CRM.

But if you are going to have decision-making-worthy math ready for the leadership team to act on, you need them to have some skin in the game when it comes to the relationships with customers. It's a hard conversation to have, and I recommend you gather allies before having it. And definitely come with a solution, not just a complaint. One way to get asked to leave the room is to come in with a problem and no solution. (Read that sentence once more. It's a good one.)

SALES CYCLE VERSUS PIPELINE VELOCITY

Let's do some defining and clarifying before we go any further. It is important to know the difference between pipeline velocity and sales cycle time. You should also have a clear point of view on what good is for each in your business.

Sales Cycle Time: The length of time it takes for a prospect to move through the entire sales process, from the initial contact (or being a stranger) to the closing of the sale. It's essentially a measure of duration. This metric is crucial for understanding how long it takes, on average, to close a deal, which in turn can help in forecasting sales and managing resources.

Pipeline: Let's start with what is likely your definition of pipeline. Pipeline is not every record in your CRM, it's only the deals or opportunities sales has accepted—or taken responsibility for—and are actively working to close. In the Revenue Engine, the pipeline actually starts in the middle of the nurture funnel, where the handoff to sales happens. We call this the MQL to SQL handoff.

Pipeline Velocity: While sales cycle time looks at the duration of the sales process, pipeline velocity is the rate at which opportunities move through the sales pipeline and are converted into revenue. Pipeline velocity is a measure of the overall health and efficiency of the sales process. A high pipeline velocity means that not only are deals moving through the pipeline quickly, but they are also of good quality (in terms of deal size and likelihood of closing). A strong pipeline velocity is an indication of a strong Revenue Engine and sophisticated go-to-market function.

 $$\textbf{PIPELINE VELOCITY} = \frac{\textbf{Number of Opportunities} \times \textbf{Average Deal Value} \times \textbf{Win Rate}}{\textbf{Length of Sales Cycle}}$$

The pipeline velocity equation helps to determine the success of your sales pipeline by measuring several key metrics. First consider the number of opportunities, which represents the total count of SQLs, deals, or potential sales in your pipeline during a specific time frame. This metric provides insight into the overall *volume* of prospects you are working with.

Next examine the average deal value, one of the three crucial Vs. Value indicates the average monetary value of the deals in your pipeline, either ARR or LTV, helping you understand the potential revenue, or *value*, each opportunity represents.

Another essential metric is the win rate, expressed as a percentage. This figure, typically provided by sales leadership, reveals the proportion of opportunities that you successfully convert into closed sales. You can also calculate this metric independently by dividing the number of won deals by the total number of opportunities in a period of time. (Am I losing you with all this math?)

Last the length of the sales cycle is a critical factor to consider. Measured in days, this metric represents the average time an opportunity takes to progress through the entire sales pipeline, from the moment it becomes a lead (awareness stage and the top of the nurture funnel) until it is successfully closed. Note: This is not tracking velocity from the first time you put them in your prospect funnel as a record, but from the top of the nurture funnel, when you have considered them an MQL. Understanding the length of your sales cycle helps you predict revenue and optimize your sales process for efficiency.

By carefully tracking and analyzing these key metrics—number of opportunities, ARR, win rate, and length of sales cycle—you can gain valuable insights into the health and performance of your sales pipeline, ultimately driving better decision-making and improved results.

WHEN DOES THE CLOCK START TICKING?

By now you know our Revenue Engine runs on math. You also know there are important decisions that you have to make that can't be made in a vacuum. They have to be made in combination with leadership and sales leadership specifically. This includes determining when the clock starts ticking.

Does the velocity clock start at the flexion point between stranger to not stranger, or does the clock start when sales accepts this lead from marketing, and says, "We're going to go close this deal"? You have many options as to when you can start the clock on your velocity, but you have to keep in mind that you can't track it if it's not a flexion point or metric or regularly tracked activity. So for example, if you were to start the clock when the sales team has their first phone call with the client, and your sales team is notorious for not tracking their activity, which happens a lot, that's not going to be a valuable or accurate way to track velocity.

I'm going to tell you a word I love: discipline. By this I mean make sure that when you are tracking velocity, the metric you choose is something that you follow and are diligent and disciplined about. Velocity is about discipline, and if your sales team is not disciplined about tracking their activity or if your marketing team is not disciplined about putting clearly qualified leads into the marketing qualified funnel, there will be many reasons why your velocity metric could be wrong.

Be sure to use a point in time that your sales cycle starts as an appropriate metric and do not let the sales team tell you it is the first time you touch that record. Remember, the first time you touch that record is not when the sales cycle starts—they are just a stranger. As I say over and over, you do not start selling to someone the first time you meet them. You don't meet someone at a bar one day and immediately ask them to marry you. (That only works in rom coms.)

So decide as a GTM team when the clock starts. This is your point of view. Then determine how long it takes your qualified prospects to close after that date. In my experience sales teams do not always love to share this with marketing. But to be fair, marketing doesn't always love to share expected outcomes of campaigns with sales either. The idea that you should ask your marketing team what to expect from a campaign (and see that come to fruition) is like asking them to look into a crystal ball. That is also the way that the sales team feels about the sales pipeline velocity. It is a secret science that only the sales team knows about, and they don't really want to commit to a number guarded as closely as Coke's recipe.

Sales and marketing need to work together (I repeat this a lot too!). But often (usually) they don't. In general sales doesn't, in my experience, like to be held accountable by the marketing team. However, again in my experience, the sales team likes to hold the marketing team accountable.

Experienced and data-driven sales leaders will wisely choose a specific point in the sales process to begin measuring deal velocity. They will regularly monitor this metric and openly share the results with the team. On the other hand, a less sophisticated sales leader will struggle in two ways: first, they won't know how to get velocity data, and second, they may make many excuses, arguing why every deal is different, and that an average is impossible to determine.

I don't necessarily recommend doing the marketing versus sales velocity. However, if you are backed into a corner, if you are given the moniker "marketing girl" like I was given back in the day, this is an opportunity for you to start measuring your own velocity, leading by example, and showing the sales team that *you can measure velocity inside your piece of the funnel.*

We're going to measure how long it takes someone to go from stranger to no longer a stranger, and then we're going to measure from the flexion point of the bottom of the prospecting funnel to the top of the nurture funnel, and then from the top of the nurture funnel to the bottom of the nurture funnel. When you deliver these metrics to the sales team, your level of insight on this topic is greater than 99.9 percent of the clients that I encounter.

This is where you can say it takes us x number of days to go from stranger to not stranger, and then it takes us x number of days to go from the top of the nurture funnel to the bottom of the nurture funnel. These velocity metrics are marketing specific.

To be clear, unsophisticated sales leaders usually come with pushback like, "The leads weren't any good." This is why the sales and marketing alignment is so important. You *can* get past that by continuing to beat the drum gently and with conviction. And if you have math to support your point of view, leadership will see your smart contribution.

Alignment between marketing and sales is an ongoing process, not a one-time fix. The three Vs—volume, velocity, and value—require continuous optimization as strategies shift. Just when you feel you have a solid understanding of the metrics and math behind your marketing automation and CRM, the leadership team may change focus to new regions or verticals. Suddenly you must rework all your models to fit the new approach. For data-driven marketers, this presents a valuable, albeit challenging, opportunity to gain deeper insights and test new strategies. This is a reality and why being adaptable is a key competency for marketers.

As a marketer you are not directly responsible for closing deals. However, by mastering the interconnected metrics and pinpointing the leading indicators that impact volume, velocity, and value, you gain significant influence. Though realignment presents more work, improving your math gives you the power to showcase marketing's impact on revenue (the only thing the board cares about). This data-savvy expertise rightfully earns you a seat at the table during key decisions, ensuring marketing strategies align with broader sales and company goals.

REVENUE ENGINE RECAP

This chapter explored the second of the three Vs (Volume, Velocity, and Value) in our Revenue Engine framework: velocity. Velocity is that elusive measurement of how quickly a deal moves through your funnels, from the initial engagement with a potential customer to the moment the deal is closed. Monitoring velocity helps you assess the effectiveness of a GTM process, identify any bottlenecks, and optimize your engagement strategies.

A few key points from this chapter:

- Velocity is measured in time, and it can only be tracked through time stamps in your CRM.

- There's an inverse relationship between velocity and value: high-value deals often have a slower velocity, while lower-value deals may move faster through the funnel.

- It's important to understand the difference between sales cycle time (the duration of the sales process) and pipeline velocity (the rate at which opportunities move through the pipeline and convert into revenue).

- Measuring velocity can be challenging, particularly if CRM usage is inconsistent or if you need advanced BI tools to analyze month-over-month changes.

- To effectively measure velocity, we need to establish a clear starting point and ensure that everyone is disciplined in tracking their activities.

- Marketing and sales teams must have alignment around a goal and work together closely to measure and optimize velocity.

I've thrown a lot at you in this chapter. Don't be afraid to read through it a few times before you go on to the next chapter on value, our third V in the Revenue Engine framework.

CHAPTER 9

THE THREE VS: VALUE

VALUE IN THE SALES PIPELINE IS BEST UNDERSTOOD WHEN WE MEASURE NOT ONLY THE IMMEDIATE REVENUE POTENTIAL BUT ALSO THE STRATEGIC FIT AND THE FUTURE GROWTH OPPORTUNITIES EACH DEAL PRESENTS.

—MIKE WEINBERG, *NEW SALES. SIMPLIFIED.*

Value is the final piece in our Revenue Engine equation. Rewind to that Girl Scout saga. Once I grasped the worth of each box and our troop's overall target, I could strategically orchestrate the volume and velocity of my cookie-peddling emails. Whether or not anyone actually appreciated that orchestration is another story. Regardless, let's explore how value catalyzes our Revenue Engine.

Value boils down to a simple equation: How much is each customer worth to your company? This ties into whether you've chosen annual run rate (ARR) or lifetime value (LTV) as your North Star (covered in depth earlier in the volume chapter). A quick reminder: ARR reflects a deal's annual run rate, or year-over-year worth, while

LTV is the lifetime value of a deal, measured by a customer's average time as a customer.

As Roland T. Rust, Christine Moorman, and Gaurav Bhalla say in "Rethinking Marketing," *Harvard Business Review,* "To compete in this aggressively interactive environment, companies must shift their focus from driving transactions to maximizing customer lifetime value."[47] LTV is a "lifetime" metric.

You must pick one metric and align your leadership team accordingly. I'm impartial on this front; the choice is yours. I'm less impartial on the discipline it takes to stick to that one metric.

Now you may recall me saying that the number of records in your prospect funnel is a moving target. With regular list hygiene (which you should be practicing), that funnel is in perpetual flux. There are flexion points as records migrate from one funnel to the next. New records enter as raw fuel before refinement. But the value of a deal in your engine should be both specific and static. It shouldn't fluctuate— you anchor your volume goals to this unwavering value.

We are going to dive into measuring value. In this chapter, we will:

- Explore why measuring value is a game changer.

- Discuss why value is one of the three vital metrics and its crucial importance.

- Reveal how pipeline value can inform strategic business decisions.

- Discover the presence of value across every funnel stage, not just the bottom.

- Examine how to leverage value to drive decision-making for your GTM function.

WHY VALUE IS SO IMPORTANT

We're keeping our definition of value tight and simple. Value in the Revenue Engine framework is just the ARR or LTV per deal. There are lots of ways to add ancillary value to a deal, but we're keeping it simple.

VALUE CAN HELP DRIVE BUSINESS DECISIONS

Measuring value in each funnel is intrinsically linked to business growth. By effectively assessing the value derived from GTM activities, you can make more informed strategic decisions, allocate resources more efficiently, and identify areas for improvement.

Understanding the value of each stage in each of the sales funnels allows for optimization of efforts where they are most impactful. For instance, recognizing high-value verticals or segments can lead to targeted marketing strategies that yield higher conversion rates and customer loyalty. Focusing on value fosters a more strategic approach that drives sustainable business growth. A clear value definition can help your GTM team deliver a closed-loop repeatable process everyone can agree on.

There's value in every stage funnel—not just the bottom of the sales funnel.

Every deal has a value, and it's not just the opportunities the sales team has identified and taken responsibility for closing. We often have to remind our clients of this. You can see in the graphic how we show it.

VALUE OF THE FUNNEL
WHERE ONE CLOSED DEAL = $100,000 ARR

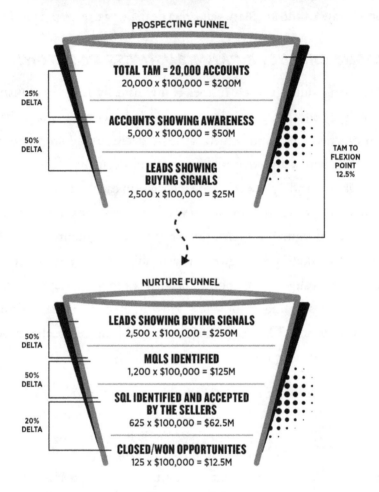

PROSPECTING FUNNEL

TOTAL TAM = 20,000 ACCOUNTS
20,000 x $100,000 = $200M

25% DELTA

ACCOUNTS SHOWING AWARENESS
5,000 x $100,000 = $50M

50% DELTA

LEADS SHOWING BUYING SIGNALS
2,500 x $100,000 = $25M

TAM TO FLEXION POINT 12.5%

NURTURE FUNNEL

LEADS SHOWING BUYING SIGNALS
2,500 x $100,000 = $250M

50% DELTA

MQLS IDENTIFIED
1,200 x $100,000 = $125M

50% DELTA

SQL IDENTIFIED AND ACCEPTED BY THE SELLERS
625 x $100,000 = $62.5M

20% DELTA

CLOSED/WON OPPORTUNITIES
125 x $100,000 = $12.5M

THE HIDDEN OPPORTUNITY COST OF MEASURING VALUE

Smaller deals might be easier and faster to close. But small deals come with the opportunity cost of losing sight of the bigger deals if you're distracted while closing the smaller deals. While smaller deals can be appealing due to their perceived lower risk and quicker closure times, prioritizing them can lead to significant opportunity costs that impact the overall efficacy of the GTM motion. Value is the key driver of good decision-making.

Aaron Ross, in *Predictable Revenue*, makes an important point: "Resist any temptation to throw in lists of random prospects just because you have them—there is an opportunity cost to marketing to poor-fit prospects."[48]

Larger deals might align more closely with a company's strategic objectives, such as entering new markets or developing relationships with key industry players. By not pursuing these deals, you may forgo opportunities that could have a significant impact on strategic direction and growth. But larger deals usually equate to more time to close than smaller deals.

Smaller (lower value) deals can be seen as low-hanging fruit: easy to close and less complex. I've seen more than one sales leader tempted to focus on small deals to quickly boost their closed/won ratios. However, this approach creates a false sense of productivity. While the sales team is busy closing a bunch of small deals, they miss more profitable and strategic opportunities. This is what I mean when I say the time and resources spent on these smaller deals are opportunity costs. The sales team could be nurturing higher-value prospects with more strategic and long-term value. Depending on your market positioning and brand perception, targeting smaller deals might position a company as a low-value provider, potentially alienating larger clients who are looking for more comprehensive solutions or strategic partnerships. This perception can limit a company's ability to attract and retain high-value clients in the future.

Like in our example earlier, larger deals typically involve a longer sales cycle with more touchpoints, providing an opportunity to build deeper relationships with clients. Strong relationships are not only vital for closing large deals but also for ensuring customer satisfaction, loyalty, and the potential for repeat business and referrals. The opportunity cost to choosing the wrong value, or not measuring it at all is the long-term value that could have been derived from deeper customer relationships.

The key is to choose a value goal per product and stick to it. Remember when I said that disqualification is just as important as any other GTM tactic? Value is the simplest disqualifier.

TYING YOUR THREE VS TO KPIS

By now you know the framework and the funnels. You understand the numbers. How do you tie your three Vs to key performance indicators to show leadership what you've got?

The easiest way to start is one KPI for each of the three Vs in each funnel. One volume KPI, one velocity KPI, and one value KPI.

VOLUME KPI

The volume KPI measures the number of new ICPs engaged and is crucial for assessing your sales team's ability to expand your customer base. Additionally, monitoring the number of new records in your CRM system monthly provides insight into the growth of your sales pipeline.

Quantifying the number of new logos engaged each month, regardless of the amount, is essential for tracking progress. You may only get four or five new logos a month, but if you add that up over a year, you should see trends and hopefully improvement.

VELOCITY KPI

Velocity KPI is all about how fast a prospect moves through your nurture funnel. You want to know the time stamp from the moment they first interact with your brand to the point where they're at the top of the funnel, ready to engage. It's the journey from "Who are you?" to "Oh, I know you now!" We call it unknown to known, then known to expert.

Another KPI is the time stamp from the top of the nurture funnel to the bottom—where the money is. This measures how long it takes for a prospect to go from being aware of your brand to actually attaching dollars to an opportunity. It's the path from "I recognize you" to "I'm ready to invest in what you're offering."

Tracking these velocity KPIs gives you a clear picture of how effectively you're moving prospects through the funnel and ultimately converting them into paying customers. It's all about understanding the speed of the journey and optimizing it for maximum impact.

VALUE KPI

The value KPI relates to the total expected revenue your deals will bring in. First, you need to have your average run rate (ARR) or customer lifetime value (LTV) locked down. Then take a look at each stage of your sales funnel and count up the number of deals in each one.

Here's where the magic happens: multiply that ARR or LTV by the number of deals in each stage, and boom, you've got the expected revenue for that particular stage. Sum up the results from all the stages and you've got your total expected revenue.

Remember your ARR or LTV will come from your sales and executive leadership team, and it should not be a moving target. You can have a chosen ARR or LTV per product, but not more than one per product. And it's not a range, it's a number. If you can't get a solid number from your leadership, then have a point of view on what it should be and stick to it. They'll see the value as you start to share your good work.

The three Vs are all leading indicators in their own right, with KPIs built in. It's where you can find the bottlenecks and where you can see what is working.

This is the start of your point of view. The point of view that gets you a seat at the table.

Importantly you now realize that marketing, sales, and revenue are all part of an integrated machine and that as a marketer you have substantial influence over optimizing this engine through strategic fueling, maintenance, and cross-team collaboration to achieve peak performance.

Let's put it all together.

Using the Revenue Engine framework we now can track volume, velocity, and value in our three funnels, prospect, nurture, and customer to see how our GTM efforts, share good news, track interest, and follow-up are working or not working.

REVENUE OPERATIONS
KPI TRACKER SAMPLE

	Marketing (Share Good News)	Prospect Funnel	Nurture Funnel	Customer Funnel	Revenue KPIs
VALUE	Site Traffic Monthly	Value of Awareness in Funnel Monthly	Value of Leads in Nurture Funnel Monthly	Value of Current Customer Up-Sell/ Cross-Sell Opportunities	Value of New SQLs Monthly
VELOCITY	Share of Voice Change (2X/Year)	Change in TAM to Lead Delta	Prospect to Nurture Flexion Point Delta Monthly	Delta in Customer Funnel	SQL to Closed/Won Delta Change Monthly
VOLUME	Activity Monthly Number of Content	Number of Net New Records in TAM	Number of SQLs Delivered to Sales Monthly	Number of Current Customers in Up-Sell/Cross-Sell Opportunity	Number of New SQLs Monthly

When this KPI dashboard is in use, you can easily see the issues in your go-to-market motions. Can you see what needs to be fixed in the KPI tracker below? What would your first step be to make changes moving forward?

REVENUE OPERATIONS
KPI TRACKER IN USE

	Marketing (Share Good News)	Prospect Funnel	Nurture Funnel	Customer Funnel	Revenue KPIs
VALUE	Site Traffic 6%	Value of Awareness in Funnel $5,000	Value of Leads in Nurture Funnel Monthly $20,000	Value of Current Customer Up-Sell/Cross-Sell Opportunities $150,000	Value of New SQLs Monthly 6%
VELOCITY	Share of Voice 2X	Change in TAM to Lead Delta 5%	Prospect to Nurture Flexion Point Delta 16%	Delta in Customer Funnel Monthly 25%	SQL to Closed/Won Delta Change Monthly 10%
VOLUME	Number of Content Pieces Monthly 10 to 15	Number of Net New Records in TAM 2,500	Number of SQLs Delivered Monthly 8	Number of Current Customers in Up-Sell/Cross-Sell Opportunity 15	Number of New SQLs Monthly 8

REVENUE ENGINE RECAP

By adjusting the three gears—volume, velocity, and value—rev your Revenue Engine and optimize your efforts, drive strategic business decisions, and foster sustainable growth.

Key points from the chapter:

- Measuring value helps make informed strategic decisions, allocate resources efficiently, and identify areas for improvement.

- Every deal has a value. Different products will have different values and require different marketing approaches.

- Focusing on smaller deals can lead to opportunity costs, such as missing out on bigger deals with more profitable and strategic opportunities. There are opportunity costs to RAOM.

- Tying the three Vs (volume, velocity, and value) to key performance indicators (KPIs) helps demonstrate the effectiveness of your GTM efforts to leadership. You can measure and track the KPIs for each of your three Vs.

- The three Vs cannot be separated from the funnels. It all works together to create the engine.

Integrating marketing, sales, and revenue into a cohesive machine and strategically measuring the value at each stage of the funnel optimizes GTM efforts and drives sustainable business growth. The volume must match the funnel, and goals should be aligned with the sales team and leadership. The value goal should be static and reevaluated yearly. The Revenue Engine framework tracks volume, velocity, and value across the prospect, nurture, and customer funnels, providing a clear picture of what's working and what needs improvement.

Next we will explore account based marketing (ABM), some sophisticated tools, and AI—all of which are transforming the way we execute a strong GTM motion.

CHAPTER 10

ACCOUNT-BASED MARKETING (ABM)

ABM IS B2B.

—SANGRAM VAJRE AND ERIC SPETT

So you've got your Revenue Engine humming along, tracking volume, velocity, and value. Your three Vs are aligned, and you're measuring what matters. The sales team is working with qualified leads and closing deals. Life is good, right? ABM is going to make it even better.

ABM is relatively new to B2B marketing. But it's not a flashy trend; it's a strategic approach that zeros in on your most valuable target accounts and treats them like the VIPs they are. You wouldn't consider spraying and praying with generic messaging. With ABM, it's all about the personalized, high-touch treatment that makes your prospects feel seen, heard, and irresistible.

Here's the thing, though, you can't just slap "ABM" on your marketing efforts and call it a day. Effective ABM requires tight alignment between marketing and sales, a deep understanding of your ICP, and the right tech stack to make the programmatic media magic happen. It's not for the faint of heart, but trust me the payoff is worth it.

ABM execution is part art, part skill, and 100 percent practice. In this chapter, we'll dive into that and more. We'll cover what it is, what it isn't, and how to make it work for your business. I've asked Crawford McCarty, one of the best marketers I've had the privilege to work with, to help me out on this chapter. Crawford is LeadCoverage's vice president of marketing and resident ABM practice leader as of this writing. You'll get insights and real-world examples, so you can see ABM in action.

By the end of this chapter, you'll have a solid grasp of how ABM fits into your Revenue Engine framework and how to rev it up to drive even better results.

WHAT ABM IS

CONTRIBUTION BY CRAWFORD MCCARTY, VICE PRESIDENT OF MARKETING AT LEADCOVERAGE

Account-based marketing (ABM) is the future of all things B2B GTM. My friend and fellow GTM pro, Sangram Vajre literally wrote the book on ABM. Twice. At first I was suspicious of ABM. "Flipping the funnel" felt silly and a little alien to me. My supply chain background tells me knowing your audience matters most, followed by a healthy dose of market awareness, and smart, targeted campaigns. But after reading all of Sangram's work as well as *No Spam, No Forms, No Cold Calls* by Latané Conant and understanding the tech stack requirements, I'm a believer.

I won't pretend I'm the first to find ABM, and I certainly won't act like this is the end-all, be-all ABM playbook—those books are written already. In fact, I just listed a few for you. This book is a primer into ABM, why you should care about it, and includes a few samples of stellar work from LeadCoverage clients that have reaped the benefits.

The American Marketing Association defines ABM as "an alternative B2B marketing strategy that works with both sales and marketing teams to treat individual prospects or customers as their own market." More simply it's marketing based on a specific customer—current or future. But this isn't about conversion rates, larger funnels, or shorter sales cycles. ABM can do all those things, sure, but ABM is really about your ROI.

Gartner says, "Strategic selling with account-based everything can drive engagement and improve conversion of targeted accounts." We agree.

WHAT ABM ISN'T

The key word in the above quote is "targeted" because it's incredibly specific and also misleading. Before I tell you why, let's talk about the modern B2B purchase life cycle.

The buying committee for B2B purchases is now often more than ten people with upward of seventy-seven touches needed to trigger buyer intent. This means you have to ask yourself, "How can I get seventy-seven touches to that committee as quickly as possible without annoying them?" You wrap them in clever marketing even though you know some of it won't "work." (Note: ABM isn't supposed to work in a traditional sense. It's not about insane conversion rates. ABM, at its core, is the tide that lifts every other ship in the harbor.)

> **ABM, AT ITS CORE, IS THE TIDE THAT LIFTS EVERY OTHER SHIP IN THE HARBOR.**

The modern buyer's journey is not what Don Draper or the other savvy executives of yesteryear so eloquently navigated. The modern buyer's journey is a self-guided tour, driven by research across several individuals, months or even years before the seller has a conversion to point to. Seventy-four percent of B2B buyers have done more than half their research online before they ever talk to a seller.[49] That means you need to make sure your team is on the list even before knowing if anyone was even taking attendance.

And with traditional methods like cold calls converting at 1 percent or less, you simply can't find a strong return on your investment without some inside help. Sure, you could get incredibly specific with your messaging and attack a vertical, subvertical, or even a specific company with the ultimate personalized touch. But how do you do that at scale without hiring an army or working every night and weekend? You don't. Don't get me wrong, targeted selling is a fantastic tool that you should absolutely utilize, but if you want to attack your whole TAM, it's not scalable.

And there's the problem with the word *targeted*. People will try to sell you the above as ABM. It's targeted selling, and it's wonderful, but it's just the appetizer.

WHAT IS INTENT

We've established that cold calls don't work, at least not as effectively as one would hope. But what about warm calls? Well, warm calls convert at about 6 percent. We're still not cooking with gas, but at least the burner's on now. You make warm calls by monitoring and reacting to buying signals like website activity or buyers' intent. Six percent doesn't sound like a huge improvement, but the math geeks at home are already giddy about that 600 percent lift and we're just getting started. If you really lean into that intent and prelude your calls with programmatic ads, you'll see your success jump to somewhere between 10 percent and 40 percent (not a typo). These are the types of results we see selling in the logistics market.

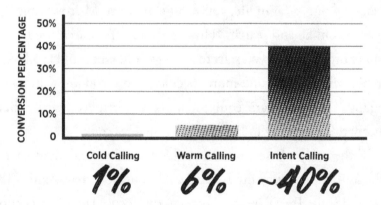

CONVERSION
EXPECTATIONS

	Cold Calling	Warm Calling	Intent Calling
	1%	6%	~40%

I know what you're thinking. I recognize that I **just** told you buyers are 50 percent or more through the cycle before they engage.

That's why intent (and your MarTech stack) is so important. Intent signals are basically your inside scoop on what's going on at your target account before they decide to tell you. I could spend hours on this and get into the extremely technical details, but all you really need to know is that intent, at a high level, is what your target is researching and reading online, whether they're on your site or not. All you have to do to see it is to buy, install, and use a tool like 6sense, DemandBase, or Terminus.

HOW WE USE INTENT

The *who* is more important than the *what* again. Knowing what your target account is researching certainly helps you identify what you should say and who you should say it to, but the real secret sauce is that intent also reveals where that prospect is in the buying cycle. It sounds creepy, but you just have to be logical. Buyers adjust what they're looking at as they better understand their needs.

Think about your own buying habits. Let's say you want to take up cooking but so far in life, you've only mastered Microwaving 101. So you go online and search, "How to cook." The search results will be super broad. But as you start to learn to boil, sauté, and broil, your searches will get more and more specific. Before you know it, you're googling "Best bain-marie equipment to cook French custard." That's a far cry from wanting to know how to merely "cook."

In the early phases, buyers probably understand they have a problem, like not knowing how to cook, but don't really know the cause or details. They'll be using broad terms focused on identification of either their pains or their executive's directives. As they become more knowledgeable, they'll identify the pain, know the solution or solutions they need, and move into researching the tools they need to either buy or partner with. This is called branded intent. At the end of the life cycle, they'll have picked a couple tools to evaluate further, and their intent will be all testimonials and case studies. Here is where the problem lies for traditional marketers. The buyer has already identified their final list before they ever revealed they were in the market.

*Graphic attributed to Latané Conant, author of *No Forms. No Spam. No Cold Calls.*

This is where a great ABM program almost seems like magic. You use intent signals to identify buyers and then place them into your engagement maturity curve. If you use the 6sense naming convention, early buyers go into the awareness stage before graduation into consideration, then decision, and finally purchase.

PROGRAMMATIC VERSUS GOOGLE

From here your only job is to simply engage with buyers before they hit decision. You could take the traditional approach and build some superspecific audiences in Google and LinkedIn, driving dynamic ads that support your email, social, and other digital channels. This is a great strategy, but it's still really lacking the scale and heavily reliant on your buyer picking you as one of their top three choices. In an industry like Logistics where there are 20,000 shippers that matter, the odds of you getting picked are astronomical without some serious PR firepower behind your brand.

This isn't a this *or* that game. This is a this *and* that game. You follow your traditional approach and then layer programmatic media buying on top of the whole thing. You serve hyper-specific ads with engagement-specific calls to action (CTAs) to your specific buyers. No, I don't mean your target list of 175 companies. I'm talking about building an ad that's going to follow Wile E. Coyote rather than just ACME Inc.

Programmatic media buying in a nutshell is serving ads to individuals at scale. And the goal of these ads isn't clicks, it's not conversions, and it's not even form fills. (Note: you'll get all of these things, and it will be exciting every time it happens, but stay with me.) The goal of these ads is to plant the seed. I tell all my clients, "Unless you work for Apple, none of your prospects wake up thinking about you." You need to create compelling ads that follow these prospects, and with the right mix of strategy and frequency, when they do graduate into that sweet spot in the buying cycle, your company will have a seat at the table.

THE APPLE EXAMPLE

Wow.

That was a lot, and I know it's a pretty big ask to hope everyone picks up what we're putting down. That's why I tell this next story. It's simple. It resonates. And without fail it sells ABM as a GTM motion.

At some point in the future, Apple is going to bring their entire supply chain in house. Strategically this makes sense to compete with Amazon. We don't know when, but I promise you every executive at every logistics company in the Apple network is waiting for the day Tim Cook gets on stage and announces it. Let's assume that day is October 20, 2026. (Note: Wouldn't it be absolutely wild if this ended up being the day it happens? I swear, this date was pulled out of thin air.)

Anyway, Tim Cook walks on stage, probably in his normal, simple outfit, and he rocks the supply chain world when he says Apple is bringing everything in house. That means he's already got vendors, partners, buyers, warehouses, trucks—everything. It has already happened. The Apple Golden Goose has already sailed. But Tim didn't make the decision to bring everything in house on that day or even a few weeks before. No, that decision was made *years* ahead of time.

Apple probably started to identify huge opportunities for growth through retail consolidation and vertical integration back in 2021, when the pandemic uncovered risks in their supply chain. There would have been a board meeting or two, and a tiger team would have been dispatched to figure out everything they need to know. The tiger team wouldn't know exactly what they needed to look for, so they'd have taken broad strokes. This is the awareness stage I referenced earlier. As they learned, they realized they needed a warehouse here and a fleet of trucks there, software to connect it all, and so on and so on. As these tiger team members were doing their research, they were sending intent signals you could capture. This was when you engage if you want to get on Apple's short list of partners.

Just like voting, ABM should be done early and often. As your target grows in maturity, your ads change to stay relevant to their needs.

WHAT GOOD LOOKS LIKE

That last bit "staying relevant" is much easier said than done.

It's easiest to break relevance down into five categories, and since this is my book, that's exactly what I'm going to do.

Engagement: You have to engage the right way. It's nailing your timing, target accounts, and personas at the finest resolution available to you. It means tailoring your approach to connect and build rapport effectively. You need to understand their specific needs, interests, and pain points so you can be the voice of authority there to guide them toward a solution at some point in the future. Your company's voice of authority comes from sharing good news.

Predictive Analysis: This is all the buzzwords. It's machine learning and AI and algorithms. These are all the things you need to at least understand to get a handle around where the market is going so you can watch and listen to the right signals. In ABM, predictive analysis is how you identify which accounts are most likely to convert and when they are likely to be "in market."

Timing: Engaging accounts at the right time is crucial in ABM. It's less about getting your ad in front of them at the exact right moment, though that is a useful skill. It means reaching out when the account is in the "in market" phase and actively seeking a solution. This requires using predictive analysis and other data-driven techniques to time your outreach effectively, after you've already built your reputation with all of your previous work.

Account-focused: ABM is account-centric. It's literally in the name, account-based, meaning it focuses on specific high-value accounts rather than broad target audiences or contacts. Engaging the right way involves understanding the unique characteristics and needs of each target account and persona and then tailoring your messaging and approach accordingly.

Persona: Understanding the personas within your target accounts is essential for effective engagement. Personas represent the different roles or individuals within an account who influence the purchasing decision. Engaging the right way means crafting messages and content that resonate with each persona's specific challenges, interests, and priorities. Note: do *not* make the mistake of aiming high here. Yes, your decision-maker might be a C-level executive, but I promise you the person doing the research on their behalf isn't. Your approach should keep both of them in mind.

MEASUREMENT AND ROI

All right, I've told you, at a high level, how to ABM. Now let's talk about my favorite part, how to measure ABM and, more specifically, find the math.

Measuring the effectiveness of ABM is delicate business. If you take the traditional approach of looking for form fills or inbound leads, you're probably going to be disappointed. ABM won't directly drive huge numbers of leads. It's not a magic bullet, rather it amplifies the impact of your campaign efforts on specific target accounts and overall business outcomes. That was a bit consultant-sounding, so put plainly, ABM drives dollars to your bottom line by itself as well as opening the aperture on everything else you do. Here are some things you can track outside of the traditional KPIs:

Account Engagement: Track metrics like website visits, content downloads, email open rates, and social media interactions for target accounts. You should benchmark how much engagement you had with an account before and after you started the campaign to track the lift.

Pipeline Velocity: Measure the speed at which target accounts progress through the sales pipeline after being engaged in the ABM campaign.

Conversion Rates: Monitor the percentage of engaged accounts that convert into opportunities and ultimately become customers.

Deal Size and Lifetime Value: Analyze whether ABM efforts are leading to larger deal sizes and higher ARR or LTV.

Customer Retention and Expansion: Assess whether ABM helps in retaining and expanding relationships with existing customers.

Account-Level Metrics: Focus on metrics specific to target accounts rather than broad, aggregate metrics. This allows you to evaluate the impact of ABM on individual accounts and tailor your approach accordingly.

Sales and Marketing Alignment: Measure the level of collaboration and alignment between sales and marketing teams. Track metrics like the number of marketing-generated leads accepted by sales, the percentage of target accounts contacted, and the speed of follow-up after engagement.

ROI and Revenue Impact: Calculate the return on investment (ROI) of your ABM initiatives by comparing the cost of the program to the revenue generated from target accounts. This provides a direct measure of the financial impact of ABM.

Attribution Modeling: Use a robust attribution model to assign value to different touchpoints and interactions along the customer journey. This helps in understanding which ABM tactics and channels are contributing most significantly to conversions and revenue.

By systematically measuring these aspects, you can develop a comprehensive understanding of the effectiveness of your ABM efforts and make informed decisions to optimize your strategy for even better results. Start small and benchmark along the way.

A NOTE ON ATTRIBUTION

Did you get all that? Now I need to tell you it all needs to be comprehensive too. The biggest gap we see with clients that are new to ABM is a missing or incomplete attribution model. This is where I insert that "no one wakes up thinking about you" analogy I mentioned earlier. If someone came to your site and filled out a form, there's a reason.

Yes, it could have been that you got lucky with an ad or a phone call, but more likely it's the impact of your target persona seeing eighty-four ads over the last twenty-nine days and deciding they should talk to your implementation team for their new capex project with a $50 million budget.

Yes, that's a real example from a client.

Yes, all the numbers are real.

Yes, we paid $0.43 to show the eighty-four ads that resulted in a $50 million deal in the pipeline.

Yes, that's a 1.1 *billion* percent return on investment.

But all of that would have been for naught had the client thought this prospect hit their website from a direct Google search despite no previous history of engagement.

BEYOND NET NEW LOGO ACQUISITION

And that's it. That's ABM.

Just kidding, there's more! The sexy approach to ABM is always net new logo acquisition. But it can do so much more. Let me break it down into a sort of "crawl, walk, run" scenario. Crawling would be having a single orchestration driving engagement across your target accounts. Walking is having multiple orchestrations that graduate prospects into the next path based on what engagement has happened. Running is when you move beyond net new logo acquisition.

ADVANCED ABM

CRAWL — Single Orchestration

WALK — Multiple Orchestrations

RUN — Competitive Listening

My favorite example is what we call "competitive listening." Technically it's not an orchestration because this one doesn't run with ads and doesn't require any budget.

Competitive listening is a targeted, intent-driven approach to your *current customer base* with a focus on retention, cross sell, and upsell. As far as complexity goes, it's actually pretty simple.

First load in your customer list or lists with as much specificity as possible. Next build an intent group largely focused on your competitor's keywords and system integrators and sprinkle some of your most applicable research signals on top based on the product that customer group has. Finally create automated alerts to notify of any surging within this group.

If your customer starts surging, one of three things is happening:

1. They have more business that you could potentially win.

2. They have a relevant need for an adjacent product.

3. They're looking to leave to go to a competitor.

In all three situations, the outcome should be the same. The account manager responsible for that account needs to reach out.

ABM helps you to create more meaningful interactions with your highest-value prospects, build stronger relationships, and ultimately drive more revenue for your business. As you move forward, remember that ABM is not a one-time campaign, but an ongoing strategic approach that evolves with your business and the needs of your target accounts.

Integrating ABM into your overall marketing efforts will not only enhance your ability to reach and convert high-value accounts but also provide a framework for continuous improvement and sustained growth. As you refine your ABM strategy, focus on aligning your marketing and sales teams, leveraging technology, and continually measuring and optimizing your efforts to achieve the best possible outcomes.

ABM is more than just a tactic; it's a comprehensive approach that can transform your B2B marketing and set your business on a path to long-term success. Plus, it's a perfect lead into a discussion on what's next in marketing technology.

REVENUE ENGINE RECAP

Once again, we covered a lot of ground in this chapter. Let's do a quick recap of the key takeaways:

1. ABM is not just a buzzword; it's a strategic approach to B2B marketing that focuses on targeted, personalized outreach to your most valuable accounts. It's about quality over quantity, folks.

2. Alignment between marketing and sales is nonnegotiable for successful ABM. (I hope you're getting bored with hearing about the relationship between marketing and sales. That would mean you've internalized it, as you should.)

3. Knowing your ICP inside and out is the foundation of effective ABM. You can't personalize your approach if you don't know who you're talking to.

4. Technology is your friend when it comes to ABM. Having the right tools in your MarTech stack can make all the difference in executing your ABM strategy at scale.

5. ABM isn't just about acquisition, it can also be a powerful tool for retention, upselling, and cross selling to your existing customers. Don't sleep on those opportunities!

6. Measuring the success of your ABM efforts requires a different approach than traditional marketing metrics. It's all about engagement, influence, and revenue impact.

ABM is not a silver bullet or a one-size-fits-all solution. It takes work, dedication, and a willingness to get up close and personal with your target accounts. It might feel a little creepy at first. But when done right, ABM can be a game changer for your business.

We're in the home stretch! Chapter eleven on AI is coming in hot. (No, I didn't use AI to write that.)

CHAPTER 11

ARTIFICIAL INTELLIGENCE AND MARKETING TECH OF THE FUTURE

AI TOOLS IN MARKETING PROVIDE DEEP INSIGHTS INTO CUSTOMER BEHAVIOR, ENABLING MARKETERS TO PREDICT NEEDS AND TAILOR THEIR STRATEGIES EFFECTIVELY.

—INSPIRED BY MARK JEFFERY, *DATA-DRIVEN MARKETING: THE 15 METRICS EVERYONE IN MARKETING SHOULD KNOW*

Though this chapter is about AI in marketing, I did not use AI to write this chapter. I did, however, ask Manoj Ramnani, CEO of SalesIntel, to help me share a point of view on AI and how it is shaping marketing technology and by extension the GTM execution.

Right now you're probably thinking, "Great, another chapter about more tech Kara wants me to master." But you would be wrong! You don't need to be a tech whiz to harness the power of AI in your marketing efforts. The best approach is to let the experts with the technology chops handle the technical aspects while you focus on being a super user of the AI-powered tools already at your fingertips. Feel better? Good!

Now, what exactly are we talking about when we say "AI"?

WHAT IS AI REALLY?

There's a lot of jargon out there, like machine learning and large language models. Here's the simplest version. AI is all about teaching computers to think and learn like humans—fast, smart, strategic, and data-driven humans. It's the ability for computers to use data to make decisions in humanlike ways, emulating deductive reasoning. And it's propelling forward at an unprecedented pace, outstripping the rapid advancements witnessed in previous technological revolutions, such as the web, social media, cloud computing, and mobile technology. With each stride forward, AI solidifies its position as the cornerstone of the fourth Industrial Revolution, reshaping societies and economies on a scale unparalleled in human history.

I'm not helping the folks in the back who are frightened that AI will take over the world, am I?

Try to relax. You're already experiencing how AI is permeating nearly every aspect of modern life, and you may not even recognize it. From personalized recommendations on streaming platforms to predictive maintenance in manufacturing, AI is already revolutionizing how businesses operate and individuals interact with technology.

Interact with a bot this week? Scanned your Netflix recommended cue? Congratulations. You've been helped by AI.

Let's do a little AI, ML, LLM 101.

Artificial intelligence (AI) is like having a supersmart computer that can learn and solve problems almost like a human. It's the brains behind things like voice assistants (think Siri or Alexa) and self-driving cars. AI uses data to understand patterns and make decisions, just like you learn from your experiences.

Machine learning (ML) is a type of AI that lets computers learn from data without being explicitly programmed. Imagine you're teaching a pet how to do a new trick by giving it treats when it gets it right. ML works similarly—it learns from examples and gets better over time. ML powers things like personalized recommendations on streaming platforms and facial recognition in photos.

While ML is a subset of AI, they are not the same thing. AI is a broader concept that encompasses any technique or technology that enables machines to mimic human intelligence, including reasoning, problem-solving, learning, and perception. ML on the other hand is a specific approach within AI that focuses on training algorithms to learn from data and make predictions or decisions without being explicitly programmed to do so. In essence ML is a tool or method used to achieve AI.

Large language models (LLMs) are like supersmart robots that understand and generate human language. They're trained on vast amounts of text from books, articles, and websites to understand language patterns and context. LLMs can answer questions, write stories, and even translate languages. They're the magic behind chatbots, virtual assistants, and tools like Google Translate.

All three are what I wish I had in college and grad school.

To illustrate the difference between the three, consider the analogy of baking a cake. AI is the goal of making a delicious cake, while ML is one of the methods you can use to achieve that goal. It's a recipe. With ML, you feed the algorithm ingredients (data), teach it how to mix them together (training), and let it learn from the process to bake the cake (make predictions or decisions).

Why should you care about robots and algorithms and cake?

Because AI is changing the game for marketing and sales. It can help you analyze customer data, personalize content, optimize pricing, and even predict future revenue. And the best part? You don't have to build these systems from scratch. And you don't need to rely on the sales team or CEO to input their data to make it work for you, unlike your CRM. The tools you already use, like your CRM, are getting AI upgrades even as you're reading this book.

In sales and marketing, AI can be applied to optimize various processes, while ML serves as a powerful tool within AI to enhance efficiency and effectiveness. For instance, AI can help companies personalize marketing campaigns to target specific audiences more accurately. ML algorithms can analyze vast amounts of customer data, such as purchasing history, demographics, and online behavior, to identify patterns and preferences. Based on these insights, AI-powered systems can recommend personalized product recommendations, tailor marketing messages, and even predict when a customer is likely to make a purchase.

Are you tingling with excitement yet? You should be. This is good stuff.

Let's put it in an example. Consider an online retailer using AI and ML to improve marketing efforts. The retailer collects data on customer interactions with its website, including products viewed, items added to the cart, and past purchases. Through ML the retailer can analyze this data to segment customers into different groups based on their preferences and buying behavior. AI-powered recommendation engines can then suggest relevant products to individual customers in real time, whether through personalized email campaigns, targeted advertisements, or recommendations on the website. By leveraging AI and ML in this way, the retailer can increase sales by delivering more tailored and compelling offers to its customers.

BECOMING AN AI SUPER USER

Manoj and I are going to date ourselves here, but consider the web twenty years ago. Prior to its invention, everyone was using desktop applications, localizing information and updates in a single file, and then distributing the file. The efficiency in collaboration that was brought about by web-based technology that allowed for the sharing of information in real time changed GTM forever. If revenue teams didn't bother to adopt these collaborative technologies, they would have simply been left behind. Similarly AI is the next wave of technology that is going to have a monumental impact on revenue generation activities.

Without getting too into the weeds, here are a few reasons why revenue teams should stay on top of AI:

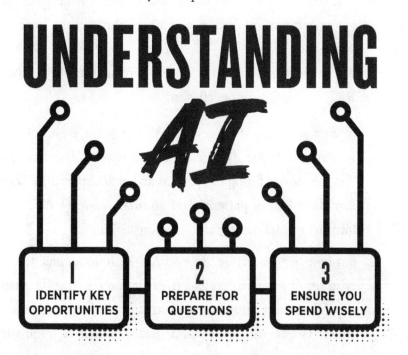

To help identify key opportunities. Once you understand the technology and how it works, you are more likely to spot the use case that will make you efficient and help you hit your revenue targets. So while AI may not help you directly hit your revenue target today, there's no doubt it's coming.

To prepare you for questions from the market. Your client may ask you if your solution is AI-enabled, and you need to be prepared to have a productive, responsive conversation about what they are looking for and why. Even if the only reason they ask is because they heard from your competitor, AI is the elephant in the room, and you can't ignore it.

To ensure you spend your own budget wisely. You are going to evaluate solutions for your teams, and vendors will make a variety of data science and AI claims. You need to be smart to differentiate reality from fiction and understand what really matters to your team's success. Not every AI implementation will make a meaningful difference to you, but you need to be able to see through the hype to identify what will.

Once you have a point of view on AI, here are four ways it can make your GTM motions more efficient:

1. In data science and processing, AI and ML algorithms can automate tasks like data cleaning, normalization, and categorization, streamlining the process and reducing errors. They can also identify patterns and anomalies within data sets, improving data quality and decision-making.

2. For content generation, AI and ML techniques enable the creation of personalized and relevant content at scale, such as product descriptions, news articles, or marketing materials. These systems can understand user preferences, linguistic nuances, and current trends to produce engaging and informative content. ChatGPT is the first iteration of this.

3. Copilot apps leverage AI and ML to assist users in various tasks, offering suggestions, predicting user actions, and providing real-time feedback. These apps can enhance productivity, creativity, and accuracy by offering intelligent recommendations and automating repetitive tasks, such as coding assistance or language translation.

4. In data analysis and insights, AI and ML models can uncover hidden patterns, correlations, and trends within large data sets, enabling businesses to extract valuable insights and make data-driven decisions. These techniques can perform complex statistical analysis, predictive modeling, and sentiment analysis, empowering organizations to optimize processes, mitigate risks, and identify new opportunities.

LEVERAGING

Data Science:	**Content Generation:**	**AI Companion App:**
• Build customer segments	• Scalable, hyper-personalization for marketing touchpoints	• Sales Companion: summarize your prospect's business, pain points, and past correspondences; ultra-fast turnaround on email/slack messages
• Intelligent pipeline analysis	• Generate beautiful, evocative imagery for marketing material, website, etc.	
• Lead scoring	• Fine-tune LLMs with domain-specific content to speak authoritatively	• Contracting Companion: Read legal documents and summarize, identify possible red flags, get advice on negotiation strategies

There's a lot of experimentation going on in this arena, and that's a good thing! Many revenue teams will get the opportunity to weigh in on proof of concepts from enthusiastic marketing technology vendors. Here are some use cases to consider that actually matter to the growth and efficiency of your team:

Enhanced Customer Insights: AI enables revenue teams to analyze vast amounts of customer data quickly and accurately. By leveraging AI-powered analytics tools, teams can gain deeper insights into customer preferences, behaviors, and purchasing patterns. This knowledge allows for more targeted and personalized ICP generation and targeting, leading to higher conversion rates and customer satisfaction.

Improved Sales Efficiency: AI automates repetitive tasks and streamlines sales processes, freeing up time for revenue teams to focus on high-value activities such as building relationships with prospects and closing deals. For example, AI-powered chatbots can handle routine customer inquiries, while predictive analytics can prioritize leads based on their likelihood to convert, enabling sales reps to allocate their time more effectively.

Optimized Pricing Strategies: AI-driven pricing optimization tools can analyze market trends, competitor pricing, and customer demand to recommend optimal pricing strategies in real time. By dynamically adjusting prices based on various factors, revenue teams can maximize profitability while remaining competitive in the market.

Forecasting Accuracy: AI algorithms can analyze historical sales data and external factors such as economic trends and market conditions to generate more accurate sales forecasts. By predicting future revenue streams more reliably, revenue teams can make informed decisions regarding resource allocation, budgeting, and strategic planning.

Competitive Advantage: In today's competitive landscape, staying ahead of the curve is crucial for revenue teams to succeed. By embracing AI technologies, teams can gain a competitive advantage by delivering superior customer experiences, optimizing sales processes, and adapting quickly to changing market dynamics. Organizations that leverage AI effectively are better positioned to outperform their competitors and drive sustainable revenue growth in the long term.

AI IN YOUR MARTECH STACK

Keep your eye out for it. Your favorite marketing tools are getting smarter every day thanks to AI. But you'll need to be careful. It's easy to get enticed by products and services that tout AI-enabled features. After all, we just spent a lot of time talking about how AI can help support revenue teams and how so many are investing in it. However, like any product, you need to go a level deeper to ensure that the product itself meets your core needs. It has to add value to your business. If the feature automates a decision or workflow that your business rarely uses, it may not be worth the effort or investment to implement. The same qualification that you always use when evaluating your tech stack still holds when evaluating AI-enabled features. Focus on ones that solve real problems for your team, automate repetitive tasks, provide actionable insights, and integrate seamlessly with your existing workflow.

Here are a few other examples of places to start with AI tools in your current MarTech stack:

Lavender. This nifty tool helps you create the best emails for your clients or your customers with personalized content, optimized subject lines, and more. Lavender helps you, through AI and LLM, create the best message for your audience, and it uses that LLM background to train itself on what the best words are to communicate with your clients or your customers.

Jasper. Imagine being able to create entire marketing campaigns from a single brief. That's Jasper—and more and more competitors in this area are emerging. You can quickly write and optimize long-form content with AI assistance and see the performance data of the content you produced. Jasper is built for teams so you can collaborate and speed up review processes across your marketing department too.

Front. Front uses AI to streamline customer communication and help your team provide top-notch service across email, live chat, SMS, and more. With real-time collaboration at its core, it enables unmatched efficiency for service teams without slowing them down like legacy help desks. Now AI is integrated across the platform to help teams deflect simple inquiries and accelerate responses to the most complex of customer challenges. They take a unique approach to infuse AI into every workflow to augment the teams supporting customers rather than replace them.

CrystalKnows. CrystalKnows analyzes millions of online data points to accurately identify a person's motivations, communication style, and other behavioral traits. They call it a personality data platform. I call it amazing. It can provide real-time recommendations based on a person's personality profile to optimize every call, meeting, and email. You can map content to their specific preferences. You can find the right words to say to the right people at the right time to have better outcomes. Maybe I wouldn't have needed a receipt on my fridge if I had CrystalKnows back then.

THE FUTURE OF AI IN MARKETING

AI is here to stay, and it's only getting smarter and more prevalent in the marketing world. But that's not a bad thing. Embracing AI now means staying ahead of the curve and gaining a competitive edge. Think of it this way: companies that were quick to adopt digital-marketing tactics like SEO and social media had a major advantage over those that stuck to traditional methods. The same will be true for AI adoption.

Yes, tech will have the ability to transform human connection. But remember, we'll continue to share good news and nurture real, live human connections at companies. After all, we are all still people, and people buy from those they trust. And if you feel like someone knows you, you are more willing to buy from them. To know someone is to research them and to really understand them, and you can't understand them unless you ask the right questions. Plus, you don't really want to be the last-standing Blockbuster brick-and-mortar in a streaming world, do you?

AI is your friend. It's not here to replace you. It's here to make your job easier and your campaigns more effective. The story of AI isn't all that different from other world-shifting technologies; the real difference is that it is here—today. Like those that embraced the internet (Netflix) versus those who ignored it (Blockbuster), we will see the same winners and losers in the next twenty years.

Here's the real takeaway: like everything else in this book, have a point of view. Read the leaders talking about AI and ML in marketing technology. Get a demo of the new and improved software hitting the market (and likely your LinkedIn inbox) every day. We're not suggesting you become an AI expert. We'll leave that to Manoj and his team. But we are saying you should come to the table with a point of view.

CONCLUSION

You did it.

You made it to the finish line! Congrats on completing your journey through the Revenue Engine framework. By now, you have the tools to earn that coveted seat at the leadership table. No more RAOM for you. You're equipped with a proven approach for delivering measurable results that will get the C-suite nodding along with you, not giving you the boot out of the room.

As we reach the end of our journey through the intricate and dynamic world of B2B marketing and sales, it's clear that the landscape has never been more challenging—or more full of potential. The strategies and frameworks presented in this book are not just theoretical constructs; they are practical, battle-tested methods designed to transform how your organization approaches growth and revenue generation.

You know now that measurable, real math can show what's working and what is not. It also shows you, your GTM team, and most importantly leadership that you have a point of view to deliver.

(And that deliverable needs to be something other than a PowerPoint deck showcasing new brand colors and a fresh tagline.) With it, you're that much closer to that seat at the table.

You're not going to get caught without a point of view. No one at the executive leadership table will be there without one. And now, neither will you.

Throughout *The Revenue Engine*, we've explored the vital components of building a high-octane Revenue Engine. Remember, it all starts with sharing good news. Not the fluff pieces, shiny websites no one visits, or vanity metrics—I'm talking real, impactful wins that move the needle, like customer successes, strategic partnerships, analysts' reports (hint, analysts are your friends), and executive thought leadership from the top brass on LinkedIn, and many other good news possibilities. The key is that all good news has to be timely, market specific, and have (yet again) a point of view.

We've examined the critical need for tracking interest, ensuring that every interaction with your audience is measured, analyzed, and optimized for maximum impact. And we've stressed the significance of follow-up, leveraging data and insights to nurture leads, and converting them into loyal customers.

I'm going to stop right there. At follow-up. I meet with customers every day. I'm on-site, at trade shows or conferences, or at speaking engagements more often than I'm at home. And without fail, when I open up the conversation to questions, I get asked, "This is great, but when does it *not* work?"

And every time I respond, "When no one does the follow-up."

Remember, you can have the hottest MarTech tools available, the cleanest lists, and the strongest data, but if there's no one following up on anything, you may as well grab yourself a Thin Mint or ten and relax. Nothing is going to happen. There has to be follow-up.

OK. Getting off my soapbox.

One of the most crucial takeaways from this book is the necessity of a shift in mindset. Gone are the days of RAOM and isolated efforts that fail to connect with the broader business objectives. Instead, we must embrace a holistic, integrated approach where marketing, sales, and customer success teams work in unison, driven by shared goals and common metrics. This alignment is the bedrock of efficient growth, enabling your organization to thrive in an increasingly competitive environment. Like follow-up, you simply have to have alignment if you're going to make any real difference, math or no math, to the bottom line.

We spent a good amount of time on the triple infinity framework: share good news, track interest, and follow up. It's more than just a methodology; it's a way of thinking that should permeate every level of your organization. By consistently applying these principles, you can build a sustainable, scalable engine that drives long-term success. (That seat at the table is getting closer and closer.)

Consider the stories and case studies I've shared. These real-world examples underscore the transformative power of a well-executed demand generation strategy. They illustrate how data-driven decision-making, combined with a relentless focus on delivering value, can propel your company to new heights. I didn't get to where I am today by writing emails. Wait. Yes, I did. And if you're a new marketer, let that be your inspiration. You can do it, too, and quicker than I did if you follow the practical steps I've outlined for you in this book.

But don't stop there. Track that interest like a bloodhound on a scent. Dial in your TAM, keep those lists squeaky clean, and zero in on the right account, not all accounts. Harness the power of your MarTech stack to capture every breadcrumb of buying intent. Because as you now know, the road to revenue is paved with buying signals from warm prospects, not cold calls to strangers.

Our three-funnel framework gives you the nuance to usher prospects from strangers to raving fans. The key is knowing when to pass the baton between marketing and sales and keeping a hawkeye on those crucial flexion points. Don't be afraid to disqualify misaligned accounts early. Your time and resources are precious.

All this strategy and activity is exciting, and I'm sure you can't wait to give it a try, but none of it matters if you're not measuring the impact. Impact through the three Vs: volume, velocity, and value. This is your North Star for proving marketing's worth. Slice and dice your CRM data to track the quantity, speed, and size of deals as they progress. Remember, revenue is the only language the board speaks fluently. In fact, to the board, it's the only language. Know these metrics intimately and wield them wisely to justify your seat at the table.

You'll need to keep your eye on the future too. AI, ABM, intent data—these tools are revolutionizing the way we engage accounts at scale. But don't get swept away by the hype and don't let AI scare you off. Ground your approach in the Revenue Engine fundamentals and layer on emerging tech where it counts. Your future self (and pipeline) will thank you.

As you move forward, remember that the journey doesn't end here. The world of B2B GTM is ever evolving, with new technologies, trends, and challenges emerging all the time. Stay curious, stay adaptable, and continue to refine your strategies based on the latest insights and best practices.

The Revenue Engine you build today is the foundation for the success you'll achieve tomorrow. It's the GPS you need to navigate the roads of B2B demand gen. Hit a pothole? It's OK. Every setback is a chance to optimize and fine-tune your approach.

SOME FINAL REMINDERS

- The *who* matters more than the what.

- Have a point of view. Make sure it's grounded in math whenever possible.

- Records are strangers.

- Avoid RAOM like you'd avoid being called the "marketing girl."

- Sales and marketing need to be aligned. Always. The Revenue Engine requires the entire team.

- Good news needs to be relevant, timely, and tracked.

- Executive thought leadership must come from a person in your company, not the corporation itself.

- Have a clear understanding of your ideal customer and the courage to disqualify prospects that don't align with it, even if they seem like attractive opportunities at first glance.

- As a marketer, you're not responsible for closing deals. But you are responsible for figuring out how the elements of measurement are working together and what is making an impact.

- Disqualification is just as important as any other GTM tactic. Value is the simplest disqualifier.

- Demand gen marketers make the best Cookie Moms.

- Sales and marketing must be aligned. Yes, I said it again. That's how important it is. Collaborate on strategy, share data and insights, and hold each other accountable if possible. When sales and marketing operate as a united GTM team, that's when the real magic happens.

So what does all this really mean? Where are we going in the future? A future where intent takes the lead?

Everything in the future will be about intent, and you will layer on intent data to this framework in the future. You'll have different sources of intent that come from your data tools like SalesIntel. It's going to come from your partners, your vendors.

Plus, there are places in every industry that will be the source of truth. And everyone who hits that source of truth is showing intent. Think about Zillow. Every human who goes to Zillow is showing intent that they want to move. Zillow and sites like it are going to be sources of intent data. I say this to stress that data providers aren't your only intent tool. In the future we'll be able to pull streams of intent from all over into one place.

And that's going to be the sexiest stuff that's going to happen in the future in my opinion.

Will you still have to share good news? Yes, you will. You'll share it with people who are showing intent, and you will follow up with them. It won't make the customer-buying journey we've talked about any easier or different. It's just going to give you more data. Remember the LEGO bricks I mentioned in the book? All this data is just going to feel like you're swimming in LEGO bricks. Streams of LEGO bricks.

Think of the houses you can build with those LEGO bricks. Zillow would have some serious competition.

But you as the marketer and GTM expert are going to have to sort through all those LEGO bricks (the data) and understand which ones are the best and why. So your whole job is going to change in the future. The role has already changed from when I started. I predict that the role will shift from creating content and putting out white papers to analyzing inbound buying signals and serving the appropriate person the appropriate content at the appropriate time—all the time.

Those of us who get there faster are going to win.

And that's what leadership wants to hear from you. They want to hear what's happening, and you need to be the expert in the room telling them.

We're on a journey together to get there taking baby steps along the way but getting there.

And that's how you get a seat at the table.

I'll see you there.

GLOSSARY

CUSTOMER FUNNEL. The journey a customer takes from initial awareness of your product or service to making a purchase, and then becoming a loyal repeat customer.

EXECUTIVE THOUGHT LEADERSHIP (ETL). The content shared by your team's leaders on platforms such as LinkedIn that shows your leadership team's expertise on important market-specific topics.

GO-TO-MARKET (GTM). Not a singular strategy but an iterative process that enables a larger strategy for your high-performing teams (marketing, sales, and customer success) to deliver a valued customer service that reinforces your brand and reflects the values and vision of your company.

IDEAL CUSTOMER PROFILE (ICP). A detailed description of the perfect customer for a business based on factors such as demographics, behavior patterns, pain points, and goals. It helps identify and target the most valuable prospects that are likely to turn into high-value, long-term customers.

INTENT DATA. A form of sales intelligence that gathers and analyzes online user behavior, such as web searches, content consumption, and digital interactions, to identify companies or individuals who are actively researching and showing interest in specific products, services, or topics.

MARKETING QUALIFIED LEAD (MQL). When a new record makes it through the prospect funnel, it becomes a marketing qualified lead when it enters the nurture funnel.

NET PROMOTER SCORE (NPS). A key metric in understanding customer loyalty and satisfaction that measures the likelihood of a customer recommending a company's products or services to others.

NURTURE FUNNEL. The marketing strategy that focuses on building relationships with prospects who may not be ready to buy, providing them with valuable content to move them closer to a purchase decision.

PIPELINE VELOCITY. The rate at which opportunities move through the sales pipeline and are converted into revenue. Pipeline velocity is a measure of the overall health and efficiency of the sales process.

PROSPECT FUNNEL. The process of attracting potential customers, educating them about your product or service, and guiding them to become a qualified lead.

RANDOM ACTS OF MARKETING (RAOM). The opposite of a strategic, respectable approach to marketing.

SALES CYCLE TIME. The length of time it takes for a prospect to move through the entire sales process, from the initial contact (or being a stranger) to the closing of the sale.

SALES QUALIFIED LEAD (SQL). When an MQL makes it through to the bottom of the nurture funnel, it is ready for closing and to become a customer.

SERVICEABLE AVAILABLE MARKET (SAM). Often presented alongside TAM, SAM is the portion of your total accessible market that is within your geographical reach.

TOTAL ACCESSIBLE MARKET (TAM). The maximum amount of revenue a business can generate by selling their products or services in a specific market.

TRIPLE INFINITY. A reminder that the work of marketing is not an event. The work of sharing good news, tracking interest in the good news, and following up on those buying signals is never done.

CONNECT WITH KARA SMITH BROWN

Kara Smith Brown lives in Atlanta, Georgia, and is pleased to connect with her readers professionally and socially!

WEBSITE: https://www.karasmithbrown.com

LINKEDIN: https://www.linkedin.com/in/karasmithbrown

YOUTUBE: @karasmithbrown

FACEBOOK: https://www.facebook.com/karasmithbrown

INSTAGRAM: @karasmithbrown.author

For professional and media inquiries, speaking engagements, and questions about *The Revenue Engine*, you can reach Kara Smith Brown directly at kara@karasmithbrown.com.

ENDNOTES

1   Soundarya Jayaraman, "Software Buyer Behavior Trends," G2 Learn Hub, April 21, 2023, https://learn.g2.com/software-buyer-behavior-trends.

2   Megan Graham, "Average CMO Tenure Holds Steady at Lowest Level in Decade," *The Wall Street Journal,* May 5, 2022, https://www.wsj.com/articles/average-cmo-tenure-holds-steady-at-lowest-level-in-decade-11651744800.

3   Spencer Stuart, "CMO Tenure Study: An Expanded View of CMO Tenure and Backgrounds," May 2023, https://www.spencerstuart.com/research-and-insight/cmo-tenure-study-an-expanded-view-of-cmo-tenure-and-backgrounds.

4   Sangram Vajre and Bryan Brown, *MOVE: The 4-Question Go-to-Market Framework* (Carson City, NV: Lioncrest Publishing, 2021).

5   Latané Conant, *No Forms. No Spam. No Cold Calls: The Next Generation of Account-Based Sales and Marketing* (Hoboken, NJ: Wiley, 2022).

6   Sangram Vajre and Eric Spett, *AMB Is B2B: Why BRB Marketing and Sales Is Broken and How to Fix It* (Washington, DC: Ideapress Publishing, 2019).

7   John Dawes, "Advertising Effectiveness and the 95-5 Rule, (linkedin.com), accessed January 22, 2024.

8   Aaron Ross and Marylou Tyler, *Predictable Revenue: Turn Your Business into a Sales Machine with $100 Million Best Practices of Salesforce.com* (Pebblestorm Press, 2011).

9   Conant, 14.

10   Conant, 48.

11   J. Romaniuk, and B. Sharp, *How Brands Grow: Part 2* (South Melbourne: Oxford University Press, 2016).

12   Council of Supply Chain Management Professionals, "The 2024 State of Logistics Report," CSCMP, accessed July 3, 2024, https://cscmp.org/CSCMP/CSCMP/Educate/State_of_Logistics_Report.aspx?hkey=bdfd8da6-e34f-434c-b39c-d3219dd4a6a2.

13   Gartner, *B2B Buying Report* (Gartner Inc., 2023), https://emt.gartnerweb.com/ngw/globalassets/en/sales-service/documents/trends/gartner-b2b-buying-report.pdf.

14   Seth Godin, *This Is Marketing: You Can't Be Seen until You Learn to See* (New York: Portfolio, 2018).

15   Gideon Gartner, *About Gartner: The Making of a Billion-Dollar IT Advisory Firm* (New York: Lemonade Heroes, 2014).

16   The 6sense Team, "How to Identify and Influence the Entire Buying Team," 6sense, accessed February 20, 2024, https://6sense.com/guides/how-to-identify-and-influence-the-entire-buying-team/.

17   "B2B Buying: How Top CSOs and CMOs Optimize the Journey," Gartner, accessed June 13, 2024, https://www.gartner.ca/en/sales/insights/b2b-buying-journey.

18   Conant, 195.

19   "How to Build Great B2B Buyer Personas," Gartner, accessed October 25, 2023, https://www.gartner.com/en/marketing/research/b2b-buyer-personas.

20   Conant, 153.

21   Scott Brinker, "Marketing Technology Landscape 2020: MarTech 5000," chiefmartec, April 2020, https://chiefmartec.com/2020/04/marketing-technology-landscape-2020-martech-5000/.

22   https://www.statista.com/statistics/1283966/number-tools-b2b-martech-stack/.

23   Donald Miller, *Building a StoryBrand: Clarify Your Message So Customers Will Listen* (New York: Harper Collins, 2017), 100.

24   "Cold Calling: What It Is & How to Do It Right," HubSpot, accessed January 6, 2024, https://blog.hubspot.com/sales/how-to-cold-call.

25   Philip Kotler, Neil Rackham, and Suj Krishnaswamy, "Ending the War between Sales and Marketing," *Harvard Business Review* (July–August 2006), accessed October 25, 2024, https://hbr.org/2006/07/ending-the-war-between-sales-and-marketing, 179.

26   Kotler et al., 189.

27   Kotler et al., 191.

28   Conant, 45.

29   Gartner, "Accelerate Efficient Growth with ABM," accessed February 20, 2024, https://emt.gartnerweb.com/ngw/globalassets/en/digital-markets/documents/accelerate-efficient-growth-with-abm.pdf.

30   J. Burton, and C. Kebler, "Demystifying Intent Data: Using Digital Clues to Accelerate Sales and Marketing Efforts," 2020.

31   Conant, 3.

32   Vajre and Spett, 21.

33   Conant, 142.

34   Conant, 142.

35   Conant, 99.

36   Aaron Ross and Marylou Tyler, *Predictable Revenue: Turn Your Business into a Sales Machine with $100 Million Best Practices of Salesforce.com* (Pebblestorm Press, 2011), 9.

37   Ross and Tyler, 60.

38   Conant, 82.

39   Conant, 160.

40   Conant, 178.

41   Conant, 130.

42   Conant, 160.

43   Conant, 145.

44   Conant, 106.

45   Gartner, "B2B Buying."

46   IBM.com, "What Is Business Intelligence?" accessed November 1, 2023.

47   Roland T. Rust, Christine Moorman, and Gaurav Bhalla, "Rethinking Marketing," *Harvard Business Review* (January–February 2010), accessed October 25, 2024, https://hbr.org/2010/01/rethinking-marketing.

48   Ross, 43.

49   Lori Wizdo, "Myth Busting 101: Insights in the B2B Buyer Journey,"
      Forrester (blog), May 25, 2015, https://www.forrester.com/blogs/15-
      05-25-myth_busting_101_insights_intothe_b2b_buyer_journey/.

9 781642 259094